Gotch vs. Zbyszko: The Quest for Redemption

By Ken Zimmerman Jr.

Gotch vs. Zbyszko: The Quest for Redemption

Copyright 2022 by Ken Zimmerman Jr.

Published by Ken Zimmerman Jr. Enterprises www.kenzimmermanjr.com

All rights reserved. No portion of this book may be reproduced, stored in a retrieval system, or transmitted in any form or by any means—electronic, mechanical, photocopy, recording, or any other—except for brief quotations in printed reviews without the prior permission of the publisher.

Published in St. Louis, Missouri by Ken Zimmerman Jr. Enterprises.

First Edition: February 2022

If you like this book, you can sign up for Ken's newsletter to receive information about future book releases. You can sign up for the newsletter and receive an e-book for signing up to the website newsletter on kenzimmermanjr.com.

Acknowledgments

This book would not be possible without the support of my family. They supported my efforts to be a published historian from the beginning. My beautiful wife Tamara is my biggest supporter despite the time commitment needed to complete these projects.

My three kids, Caity, "Trey," and Caleb provide a sounding board for my ideas and provide feedback on story and cover design. I taught all of them martial arts. They have taught me more than I taught them.

For my two grandchildren and counting, you are my inspiration. Papa loves you.

Table of Contents

Introduction 8

Chapter 1 – Frank Gotch in 1909 12

Chapter 2 – Stanislaus Zbyszko Arrives in America 40

Chapter 3 – Zbyszko Tours the United States 51

Chapter 4 – Zbyszko's Tour Continues 75

Chapter 5 – World Title Match 94

Chapter 6 – Gotch Wants One More Pay Day 109

Chapter 7 – Zbyszko Presses for Rematch 117

Chapter 8 – Continuing to Pursue Gotch 133

Chapter 9 – Zbyszko Returns from His Summer Vacation 144

Chapter 10 – Frank Gotch Retires 167

Chapter 11 – Zbyszko Returns to Europe in 1914 176

Conclusion 191

Epilogue 196

Other Combat Sports Books by Ken Zimmerman Jr. .. 202

Bibliography 203

About the Author 209

Endnote 211

Introduction

I wrote *Gotch vs. Hackenschmidt: The Matches That Made and Destroyed Legitimate American Professional Wrestling* to document Frank Gotch's two most important matches. Going into the project, I was a fan of Georg Hackenschmidt but not Frank Gotch. After researching the matches and incidents leading up to both, I developed an abiding respect for Gotch.

While these matches were the biggest of Gotch's career, Georg Hackenschmidt was not his toughest opponent. Stanislaus Zbyszko and Tom Jenkins hold the distinction as Gotch's most dangerous opponents. Gotch wrestled Jenkins multiple times throughout his career. Gotch wrestled Zbyszko in one legitimate contest and refused to wrestle him ever again.

This book looks at the circumstances leading up to the contest, the actual match and Zbyszko's desperate attempts to secure a rematch. Even after Gotch's retirement in 1913, Gotch belittled Zbyszko's abilities to deny Zbyszko championship recognition from the fans and cover up for Gotch's refusal to wrestle him again.

This book begins in 1909. In the previous year, Frank Gotch defeated Georg Hackenschmidt for the world title on April 3, 1908. Gotch made two title defenses against familiar foes, Hjalmar Lundin, and Dr. Ben Roller. He then left for a vaudeville tour of London. Gotch started seriously defending his title in 1909.[i]

As 1909 began, Stanislaus Zbyszko was still in Europe. Zbyszko traveled to the United States in late 1909 for the express purpose of securing a title match with Gotch. In June 1910, Gotch and Zbyszko wrestled the most significant title match since Gotch took the title from Hackenschmidt.

Figure 1-Stanislaus Zbyszko from a 1910 edition of the St. Louis Post-Dispatch (Public Domain)

Chapter 1 – Frank Gotch in 1909

Frank Gotch defended his title for the first time in 1909 on March 25th. Gotch's manager, Emil Klank, and trainer, Martin "Farmer" Burns, booked the match in Kansas City, Missouri. Unlike previous wrestling champions, who preferred bigger cities like New York City, Gotch primarily wrestled in the Midwest.

Gotch and Burns viewed the Midwest as a hotbed of wrestling. Midwestern fans rewarded their faith by turning out in large numbers to see Gotch defend his championship. While Gotch, Klank, and Burns normally booked the biggest matches in Chicago, Gotch frequently wrestled in Kansas City, Missouri, Omaha, Nebraska, and Des Moines, Iowa.

11,000 fans crowded into Kansas City's Convention Hall to see Gotch defend his title against "the Pride of France", Raoul de Rouen.[ii] The 26-year-old de Rouen was also known as "Raoul the Butcher". De Rouen was a good journeyman wrestler, who defeated Hjalmar Lundin and Charley Olson.[iii]

Gotch defeated de Rouen easily. Gotch pinned de Rouen with a reverse half-Nelson for the first fall in 34 minutes, 34 seconds.[iv]

Gotch took the second fall in dominating fashion. Gotch took de Rouen to the ground and applied his toe hold. De Rouen submitted quickly to avoid Gotch hurting him with Gotch's pet hold.[v] Gotch took the second fall in only 13 minutes.

Gotch wrestled John Perrelli the following night in Omaha, Nebraska. He must have left the match with de Rouen and immediately boarded a train for Omaha.

When Gotch wrestled back-to-back matches, he often wrestled a "worked" match in one or both matches. However, in this instance, Burns just matched him against inferior wrestlers. Gotch dispatched de Rouen handily but played with Perrelli.

Perrelli knew Gotch was superior, so he tried to out foul Gotch, the foul master. Usually, Gotch applied a submission hold on the miscreant and seriously injured him. Gotch took Perrelli's challenge so lightly that he settled for embarrassing Perrelli.

Perrelli charged at Gotch to start the bout, but Gotch grabbed Perrelli around the waist. With a heave, Gotch tossed Perrelli through the ropes. Perrelli threw a punch at Gotch, who smiled at Perrelli's weak attempt at retribution.[vi]

Gotch openly mocked Perrelli through the remainder of the bout further infuriating his challenger. After tossing Perrelli through the ropes two more times, Gotch slipped behind Perrelli. Using his superior position, Gotch applied a reverse half-Nelson. Gotch flipped Perrelli onto his back for the first fall at 11 minutes, 15 seconds.[vii]

Gotch further embarrassed Perrelli by securing the toehold twice but releasing it before applying any pressure. Perrelli connected on a punch under Gotch's left eye, which caused a small cut. Gotch started to get mad but laughed it off and ruffled Perrelli's hair. Tiring of messing with the young challenger, Gotch picked

Perrelli up with a body hold and pushed his shoulders into the mat for the second fall after 10 minutes.[viii]

Gotch released Perrelli and held out his hand. Perrelli swung a punch at Gotch, who side stepped the blow. After fans began booing Perrelli, he calmed down and shook Gotch's hand.[ix]

Perrelli did not realize how lucky he was. Gotch normally hurt someone who punched him. Gotch's good humor saved Perrelli injury and a long recovery.

Figure 2-Frank Gotch from the Star Tribune of March 28, 1909 (Public Domain)

Gotch needed to be serious for his next title match. Gotch defended his title against Yussif Mahmout on April 14, 1909, in Chicago, Illinois.

Burns, Klank and Gotch continued their practice of booking their biggest matches in Chicago.

Antonio Pierre, Mahmout's manager, billed Mahmout, a Bulgarian, as the "Terrible Turk." After the original "Terrible Turk," Yusuf Ismail, successfully toured America in 1898, a fair number of wrestlers employed this gimmick. St. Louis promoters even matched a "Terrible Turk" against World Heavyweight Wrestling Champion Georg Hackenschmidt when he toured America in 1905.

Mahmout wrestled bare foot and requested not to wear wrestling shoes for the match with Gotch.

After agreeing to forfeit $500 to Gotch, Gotch's camp agreed to allow Mahmout to wrestle bare foot.[x]

Gotch would have a harder time applying the toehold without the friction of a wrestling shoe which afforded a better grip. A sweaty leg and foot slips the toehold grip easier.

10,000 fans crowded into the Dexter Park Pavilion to watch the match.[xi] Four matches made up the card, but everyone came to see Gotch defend his title.

Gotch and Mahmout entered the ring at almost 11:00 p.m. They shook hands at 10:57 p.m. and referee Ed Smith, the Sporting Editor of the *Chicago American* as well as frequent referee of Gotch's matches, started the match.

Gotch stood five feet eleven inches tall, three inches taller than Mahmout. Mahmout, built like a fire plug, appeared to have the strength advantage, but Gotch was fifteen pounds heavier at 210 pounds. If Mahmout possessed a strength advantage, he did not use it effectively.

Gotch probed Mahmout's defenses with straight arm pushes to Mahmout's head and shoulders. Gotch grabbed a waist hold, took Mahmout off his feet and slammed him to the mat. Mahmout scurried back to his feet, but Gotch grabbed a single leg takedown and dumped Mahmout back to the mat.[xii]

Mahmout got back to his feet and attempted a front face lock on Gotch. Gotch used both hands to push Mahmout's hips away from him as he used his upper body to fling Mahmout to the side. Mahmout fell to his knees but jumped back to his feet.[xiii]

Gotch secured another waist hold but Mahmout grabbed the ropes during Gotch's lift causing Gotch to release his grip and fall to his butt.[xiv] Before Mahmout could do anything, Gotch scrambled to his feet.

On his way back to his feet, Gotch locked his arm around Mahmout's leg picking him up off the mat and dumping him to the floor. Before Mahmout could turtle up, Gotch secured a half-Nelson and crotch hold.[xv] Gotch flung Mahmout over to his back.

Mahmout reached for the ropes in a desperate attempt to prevent the fall, but referee Smith warned him to release the ropes. In this era, the ropes did not cause a break in the action. Gotch pushed

Mahmout's shoulders to the mat for the first fall in eight minutes.[xvi] The pro-Gotch crowd cheered the champion for ten minutes, longer than it took Gotch to defeat Mahmout.

After the 15-minute intermission, the men met at center ring to restart the match at 11:27 p.m.[xvii] Mahmout tried to press the action, but it was apparent to the fans that Gotch would win the title match.

Mahmout attempted three single leg takedowns.[xviii] Each time, Gotch kept his leg pressed to the floor and broke Mahmout's grip.

Mahmout finally drug Gotch to the mat with an arm drag. Gotch ended up on his hands and knees. Mahmout tried to turn Gotch but could not. In an act of desperation, Mahmout grabbed Gotch around the waist and tried to lift him off the mat. Gotch entangled his legs with Mahmout to prevent the lift and then flipped Mahmout off him.[xix]

Gotch lifted Mahmout off the mat with a single leg takedown and dumped him to the floor. Gotch followed grabbing Mahmout's foot for the toehold. Fortunately for Mahmout, his sweaty foot allowed him to slip Gotch's pet hold.[xx]

Mahmout's escape amused Gotch, who secured a hammerlock, while Mahmout was on his hands and knees. Mahmout flung himself out of the ring to escape the pain of the hammerlock.[xxi]

Smith ordered the men back to the center of the ring. Mahmout refused to allow Gotch to put the hammerlock on. Smith appealed to Mahmout's manager Pierre to convince Mahmout to allow Gotch to reapply the hammerlock. If Mahmout still refused, Mahmout would force Smith to disqualify him.[xxii]

Gotch stood in the corner smiling, while the drama over the restart occurred. Mahmout finally went back to his hands and knees allowing Gotch to reapply the hammerlock. However, as soon as Smith restarted the match, Gotch released the hold and allowed Mahmout back to his feet.[xxiii] Gotch knew his title was safe. Mahmout was not on Gotch's level.

After taking Mahmout to the mat three separate times with the half-Nelson and crotch hold, Gotch switched to a reverse Nelson. Gotch flipped Mahmout to his back and pinned him a second time in 9 minutes, 10 seconds.[xxiv] Gotch defended his title with a dominating win in two straight falls.

Figure 3-Artist Rendering of Gotch wrestling Mahmout from the April 15, 1909, Chicago Tribune (Public Domain)

The defeat left Mahmout dejected. He told reporters that he planned to return to Bulgaria for the summer before returning to the United States later in 1909.[xxv] He said he might seek a rematch with Gotch, but he was not sure.

Mahmout wrestled in the United States off and on for the next three years.[xxvi] In 1911, Gotch selected Mahmout as one of the men along with Zbyszko and Hackenschmidt, who should wrestle each other to determine the next challenger for Gotch. Both Zbyszko and Hackenschmidt detested Mahmout from their time in Europe and adamantly refused to wrestle him. Gotch eventually wrestled Hackenschmidt in 1911.[xxvii]

Gotch finished out April with a couple title matches against former opponents. On April 20th, he wrestled Dan McLeod, the former American Heavyweight Wrestling Champion. Gotch beat McLeod in two straight falls. It took Gotch 18 minutes, 20 seconds to secure the first fall. Gotch won the second fall in only 5 minutes, 16 seconds.[xxviii]

In what amounted to little more than a public workout, Gotch wrestled Ben Reeves in Boone, Iowa. Gotch three Reeves three times in under an hour.[xxix] It only lasted that long because Gotch was taking it easy on the inexperienced wrestler.

Burns booked Gotch for a big match in one of their regular venues, the Convention Hall in Kansas City, Missouri. 5,500 fans showed up to see the champion defend his title.[xxx]

Promoters would normally be ecstatic to see a crowd of this size during the first decade of the Twentieth century. However, Kansas City wrestling cards often drew eight to ten thousand fans per card. The smaller crowd disappointed the wrestlers, who anticipated a big payday in Kansas City.

Gotch wrestled Dr. Benjamin Roller in Kansas City. Gotch beat Roller every time they met but admitted Roller always provided a tough challenge.

Gotch defeated Roller in two straight falls. Gotch won the first fall in 37 minutes, 55 seconds with a half-Nelson and crotch hold. Gotch used a reverse Nelson to win the second fall in 18 minutes, 29 seconds.[xxxi]

Gotch's last opponent in April was Charles Hackenschmidt. Hackenschmidt won the World Light Heavyweight Wrestling Championship under his real name, John Berg. Gotch wrestled Hackenschmidt in Memphis, Tennessee on April 29th.

Berg possessed above average skill, but his lack of size hampered him in matches with large heavyweights like Gotch. The men agreed to handicapped conditions, where Gotch won the match if he defeated Young Hackenschmidt three times in an hour.

1,500 fans showed up to see the champion demonstrate his skills. Gotch took Hackenschmidt (Berg) to the mat after about 10 minutes. "Watch out for your foot," Gotch told Hackenschmidt, who submitted before the hold damaged his ankle.[xxxii]

Gotch ended the second fall even more quickly. He secured the toehold after seven minutes. He forced Hackenschmidt to submit again.[xxxiii]

After a second 10-minute intermission, Gotch only needed three minutes to end the third fall with his toehold.[xxxiv] Gotch was dominating his competition.

Gotch traveled to Denver, Colorado in early May to wrestle old foe, Fred Beell, in a worked match. Gotch defeated Beell in twenty-four minutes with his toehold.[xxxv]

The fans noticed Gotch was carrying Beell. They booed him and told him to "get on with it." Gotch slammed Beell for the second fall and match in three seconds.[xxxvi]

Gotch wrestled another public workout in a handicap match with Ed Ferguson and M. Yokel in Salt Lake City, Utah on May 21, 1909.[xxxvii] Fans only attended these matches to see Gotch's greatness.

In another handicapped match, this time in Sioux City, Iowa, Gotch wrestled Oscar Wasem, formerly of St. Louis but now wrestling out of Nebraska. Kubiak, the Bohemian Giant, was the second wrestler to face Gotch. Gotch pinned Wasem twice and Kubiak once to take the victor.[xxxviii]

Early in his career, Gotch held the Iowa Championship, while Wasem was the St. Louis Champion. They wrestled a champion versus champion match in 1901. Wasem defeated Gotch in a one fall match. However, Gotch beat Wasem in 1902. After the 1901 defeat, Gotch beat Wasem every time they wrestled.

Gotch wrestled another handicapped match in Sioux Falls, South Dakota. Gotch defeated Dan McDonald, Joe Ackron and Professor Miller.[xxxix]

Gotch agreed to wrestle his greatest rival, Tom Jenkins, in Des Moines, Iowa on June 14, 1909. In preparation for this match, Gotch wrestled Henry Ordeman in Minneapolis, Minnesota on June 3, 1909.

Gotch and Ordeman may have worked this match. Gotch trained Ordeman early in his career. It is difficult to tell with this match.

Gotch won the match in straight falls. Gotch won the first fall in twenty-six minutes with a scissors and bar arm hold. Gotch won the second fall in ten minutes with the same hold.[xl] If the men were not working with each other, the match was a friendly contest.

Frank Gotch wrestled his old rival, Tom Jenkins, one of the few men to hold multiple wins over Gotch. 7,000 fans crowded into the Des Moines Pavilion to see the contest.[xli]

Figure 4-Tom Jenkins circa 1905 (Public Domain)

Gotch announced to the newspapers before the match that he would not be wrestling anymore matches in 1909. In November, he changed those plans to publicize a big match with a foreign newcomer. At the time of the Jenkins match, he planned to take it easy the rest of the year.

37-year-old Jenkins was five years older than Gotch. Jenkins semi-retired in 1905 to teach self-defense at the U.S. Military Academy at West Point. He only wrestled part-time for the next four years but his stellar record with Gotch earned him this match.

In previous matches, Gotch and Jenkins fouled each other freely. Fans anticipated another rough contest, but the passage of time changed how Gotch saw Jenkins.

Gotch only fouled when he was worried about losing a match. Gotch knew Jenkins was no longer his equal, so he did not need to foul.

The men met at center ring, shook hands, and took their corners.

When they met at center ring, 37-year-old Jenkins was not five years older than Gotch. When they met in the ring this time, Jenkins appeared a decade older.

Jenkins scored his only offense in the first five minutes of the match. He slipped behind Gotch, who sat down on the mat in a defensive position. Jenkins worked to turn Gotch but could not move the champion. After a minute, Gotch spun out of danger and was back on his feet facing Jenkins.[xlii]

Gotch picked up Jenkins and slammed him to the mat. Gotch backed off and allowed Jenkins to scramble back to his feet.[xliii] Gotch repeated the process two more times. Fans heard a sickening thud every time Jenkins hit the mat.[xliv]

After the third slam, Gotch put a reverse Nelson on the dazed

Jenkins. After a minute, Gotch forced Jenkins on to his back for the first fall at fourteen minutes, twenty-eight seconds.[xlv] The men retired for a ten-minute intermission.

To start the second fall, Jenkins grapevined Gotch's leg. Both men fell to the mat, but Gotch was on top. Gotch slammed Jenkins twice to the mat, while Gotch was on his knees. Jenkins grimaced after each throw. Gotch pinned Jenkins with a crotch hold and half Nelson combination in only 7 minutes, 53 seconds.[xlvi]

After the match, Gotch hinted at retirement. The rumors really picked up steam a week later, when Gotch checked into a St. Louis hotel, the Planters, as "Frank Gotch and wife."[xlvii] Newspaper reporters did not identify his wife by name but said she was a Chicago telephone operator. Gotch and "his wife" reported they were traveling to Hot Springs, Arkansas for their honeymoon. The story appeared in dozens of newspapers across the country.xlviii

However, Gotch did not marry until 1911. A couple of newspapers printed the name of Gotch's reported fiancé, but I am omitting it from this narrative. We are not sure who Gotch booked into a room in St. Louis.

The incident does show Gotch's mindset at the time. Gotch intended to rest for the remainder of the year.

Gotch spent the summer in Iowa as his manager tried to lure Georg Hackenschmidt back to the United States. Hackenschmidt refused to return unless Gotch's team guaranteed him $12,000, whether "Hack" won, drew, or lost the rematch with Gotch.[xlix]

Gotch told his manager that Hackenschmidt's asking price was too high. He continued his Iowa vacation with the intent of staying home until 1910. The arrival of a celebrated Polish wrestler ended his vacation and led to his first serious challenge since the first match with Hackenschmidt in 1908.

Figure 5- Frank Gotch circa 1909 from the Commercial Appeal (Public Domain)

Chapter 2 – Stanislaus Zbyszko Arrives in America

Because Gotch was such a dominant champion, Gotch's manager Emil Klank frequently looked to oversees talent to increase interest in Gotch's title defenses. Klank reasoned a fresh talent, who fans had not seen, had an easier time convincing the paying customer they had a chance to beat Gotch.

Gotch set his eyes on a rematch with Hackenschmidt because it was the most lucrative bout available. However, Hackenschmidt proved to be a difficult negotiator.

Klank discovered another celebrate European wrestler during the summer of 1909. Stanislaus Zbyszko, born Stanislaus Cyganiewicz on April 1, 1880, in

Poland, won Greco-Roman wrestling tournaments in Europe during 1908 and 1909.

Standing five feet, nine inches tall and weighing 245 pounds, Zbyszko resembled a beer keg with arms and legs. A visually impressive wrestler, Zbyszko's physique alone would peak fan interest in a potential Gotch title defense.

Klank approached Zbyszko's handlers, who showed interest in travelling to the United States for a match with Frank Gotch. Zbyszko hired J.H. Herman, a manager and promoter from Buffalo, New York, to represent him in the United States.[1]

Figure 6-1909 Newspaper Photograph of Stanislaus Zbyszko from the Library of Congress (Public Domain)

Klank may have recommended Herman as Buffalo, New York was the site of the match establishing Zbyszko as a serious challenger to Frank Gotch.

Zbyszko booked passage on a ship scheduled to dock in New York City on September 17, 1909.[li] Zbyszko planned to wrestle a tour of the United States in early 1910 leading to a summer title shot with Frank Gotch.

On November 14, 1909, Herman announced Frank Gotch signed to wrestle Stanislaus Zbyszko in a handicapped match on Thanksgiving night, November 25th, at Buffalo.[lii] To prepare for the match, Gotch had cut his vacation short.

On November 6, 1909, Gotch toyed with Frank Prindle in a handicapped match in Chicago. He pinned Prindle twice in thirty minutes, but reporters said Gotch carried Prindle. They wrote that Gotch could have pinned him thirty times in the thirty minutes.[liii] If his next challenge were not more difficult, his challenger was at least a recognized name.

Figure 7- Giovanni Raicevich from a 1909 newspaper in the Library of Congress (Public Domain)

Giovanni Raicevich killed two opponents in Italy if you can believe the pre-match hype. While promoters often made these stories up, Raicevich looked like he could kill someone. Raicevich developed a bodybuilder's physique during a time, where fans rarely saw heavily muscled men.

Klank imported Raicevich to wrestle Gotch, but Raicevich did not have the reputation of Hackenschmidt or Zbyszko. Still, 15,000 Chicago wrestling fans turned up to watch Gotch defend his title.[liv]

Gotch demonstrated his superior wrestling skills against Raicevich, who appeared scared to engage with the champion. As soon as the referee started the match, Gotch grabbed a single leg takedown and dumped Raicevich to the mat.[lv]

Gotch secured a toehold, which normally ended the match. Surprisingly, Raicevich squirmed out of the hold. As shocked fans gasped, Gotch simply smirked and went back to work.[lvi]

Raicevich perspired freely, which helped him defensively for the first ten minutes. Raicevich also slipped out of Gotch's crotch hold and half-Nelson combination.[lvii] Besides the toehold, this combination won countless matches for Gotch over his career.

Raicevich slipped the moves but only delayed the inevitable. Gotch slung Raicevich back to the mat and grabbed his waist before Raicevich could get to his feet. Gotch applied a crotch and bar arm hold. Using the hold to turn Raicevich to his back, Gotch pressed his bodyweight on Raicevich pinning him to the mat. Gotch won the first fall at 16 minutes, 28 seconds.

Gotch wasted no time on the second fall. He pushed Raicevich around the ring for two or three minutes before dropping him back to the mat with a single leg takedown. Gotch twisted Raicevich into a cross leg, hammer, and wrist lock to take the second fall in five minutes, 28 seconds.[lviii] Gotch was ready for Zbyszko.

Before he left for Buffalo, process servers delivered a summons to Gotch for a breach of promise suit. Another girl from Chicago, not named as his fiancé earlier, sued him for a broken marriage proposal.[lix]

Gotch wrestled Dr. Benjamin F. Roller in front of about 5,000 fans in Kansas City on November 15, 1909. Gotch again won in two straight falls.[lx]

Gotch travelled to Buffalo for the Thanksgiving night match. He agreed to throw Zbyszko twice in one hour or lose the match.[lxi]

It was unusual for the champion to accept these terms, but the crowd was as confident as Gotch that he would win. The crowd bet heavily on Gotch in the handicap match.[lxii]

Zbyszko surprised the champion and the crowd by wrestling defensively. Gotch did take Zbyszko down and apply the toehold at one point. However, the barefooted Zbyszko pulled his foot from danger. Gotch could not throw Zbyszko once before the hour time limit expired.[lxiii]

While the setback did not affect Gotch's title reign, it did make him look vulnerable for the first time in a while. If Zbyszko wrestled to win instead of not to lose, could he have beaten Gotch? Promoters seized on this question to publicize the title match in the summer of 1909. It was the perfect setup for a big match.

Because this match was the perfect segue to a title match and the fact that Gotch's title was not on the line, I believe that Gotch and Zbyszko worked this match to build up the title match in the summer. It was dull enough to be a contest.

Zbyszko spent the next six months touring the United States to prepare for the title shot with Gotch. Zbyszko dropped from as high as 260 pounds to his peak weight for the match of 227 pounds. Fortunately, Zbyszko's hard schedule did not sap his strength, one of his biggest assets in a match with Gotch.

Gotch on the other hand entered the most inactive period of his career. He wrestled only two matches before answering the challenge of Zbyszko in June 1910. Was Gotch making a mistake?

Figure 8-Stanislaus Zbyszko from the Boston Globe in May 1913 (Public Domain)

Chapter 3 – Zbyszko Tours the United States

Stanislaus Zbyszko began his wrestling tour in Iowa and Minnesota during December 1909. Zbyszko had six months to get in shape for his challenge of Gotch.

Zbyszko wrestled few great wrestlers during this tour. The matches served as workouts to get him in peak condition. Herman also wanted to familiarize the American wrestling fans with Zbyszko. The tour provided an opportunity for fans across the United States to see Zbyszko in action.

Zbyszko wrestled a typical tour match on Tuesday, December 14, 1909, at the Towle Opera House in Davenport, Iowa.[lxiv] Promoters chose local wrestler Rauol de Boulanger as Zbyszko's opponent.

Zbyszko applied a body hold on de Boulanger and slammed him to the mat twice to win the match in two straight falls. Zbyszko won the first fall in 5 minutes, 5 seconds. He won the second fall in 6 minutes, 18 seconds.[lxv]

On Thursday, December 16, 1909, Zbyszko wrestled a stronger competitor in Henry Ordeman. Zbyszko agreed to throw Ordeman twice within the one-hour time limit. If Zbyszko failed to throw Ordeman twice, the referee would award the match to Ordeman.[lxvi]

In a recent match, Ordeman stifled Frank Gotch's offense, so fans saw Ordeman as a challenge for Zbyszko. Gotch and Ordeman worked that match though as Ordeman was Gotch's protégé. A "large crowd" turned out to see the match.[lxvii]

The men tied up in the center of the ring with both men looking for an opening. Ordeman scored first taking Zbyszko to the mat with a double leg takedown. Zbyszko squirmed away but Ordeman stayed glued to Zbyszko's back.[lxviii] Zbyszko finally turned and stood up to escape the danger.

Zbyszko spun to Ordeman's back, took Ordeman off his feet with a back body hold and tried to turn Ordeman. Ordeman escaped Zbyszko's pin attempt.[lxix] The men remained on their feet for the next thirty minutes.

Zbyszko dove for a single leg takedown after the thirty-minute mark and took Ordeman to the mat. Zbyszko tried turning Ordeman again, but Ordeman reversed position.[lxx]

Ordeman attempted a toehold, but a sweaty Zbyszko was able to pull his bare foot free.[lxxi] Zbyszko eschewed wrestling boots whenever he could preferring to wrestle bare foot.

At the fifty-minute mark, Zbyszko asked the referee to allow both men to towel off as both men were sweating profusely.[lxxii] The perspiration interfered with the men securing a hold or even obtaining a solid grip. The referee told him to continue wrestling.

Ten minutes later, the referee called the match and raised Ordeman's hand since Zbyszko did not meet the agreed upon stipulations.

The result might have hurt Zbyszko's standing as a contender, but Ordeman's success with Gotch in worked matches blunted the criticism of Zbyszko. After the match, Zbyszko praised Ordeman's skill allowing that he may have taken Ordeman lightly.[lxxiii]

On Christmas Eve, Zbyszko was in Ottumwa, Iowa to wrestled George Turner.[lxxiv] Zbyszko agreed to throw Turner three times in one hour or Turner would win the match.[lxxv]

Turner proved quicker than Zbyszko, who had to chase Turner down to put a hold on him. Zbyszko secured his body hold three times and took Turner to the mat, but Turner broke the waist lock and escaped each time.[lxxvi]

Zbyszko finally gave up on the body hold. He grabbed an arm bar on Turner's right arm, lifted him off the ground and dumped him to the mat. Turner landed on his right shoulder. As his right arm hung limp, Zbyszko pushed Turner's shoulders to the mat.[lxxvii]

During the intermission, a doctor examined Turner and told him he could not go on. It would take a month or more for Turner's shoulder to heal. Turner expressed a desire to wrestle Zbyszko again.[lxxviii]

Zbyszko scored a decisive win over Turner but the reporter for the *Ottumwa Tri-Weekly Courier* was not impressed. He opined that Zbyszko was too slow to beat Gotch.[lxxix] Zbyszko had six months to change observers' minds about his chances with Gotch or suffer a lack of interest at the box office+.

Zbyszko suffered another setback in Des Moines, Iowa on December 27, 1909. Herman booked Zbyszko to wrestle three men, all of whom Zbyszko agreed to throw in one hour. Zbyszko crushed James Corbin in 3 minutes, 10 seconds. However, the second man, Jesse Reimer, wrestled Zbyszko for the remaining hour without Zbyszko scoring another fall.[lxxx]

Figure 9-Jess Westergaard from the Library of Congress Collection (Public Domain)

Reimer represented a bit of a trap for Zbyszko. Reimer usually wrestled as Jess Westergaard. Martin "Farmer" Burns trained him for the ring. Gotch wrestled Westergaard often in preparation for big matches. Westergaard's skills improved during the time he was Gotch's main sparring partner.

Westergaard was a world title contender throughout the 1910s. Burns and Gotch may have sent Westergaard, who was from Des Moines, to bring them intelligence on Zbyszko's style and tendencies.

Zbyszko continued touring in January. Herman must have been pushing him to put on more dominant performances. Herman got his wish four days later.

On New Year's Day 1910, Zbyszko was back in manager Herman's hometown of Buffalo, New York. Herman booked Zbyszko to wrestle former American Heavyweight Wrestling Champion Fred Beell.[lxxxi] Defeating Beell would go a long way in establishing Zbyszko as a serious challenger for Gotch.

Zbyszko enjoyed a significant size advantage over Beell. Zbyszko stood only five feet, nine inches but he was about four inches taller than Beell. At his lightest, Zbyszko weighed 227 pounds. He weighed around 245 for this match. Beell weighed 165 pounds at his heaviest.

Figure 10 - Fred Beell, a powerful but small wrestler possessing world class wrestling skills but often hampered by his lack of size (Public Domain)

Beell beat larger opponents throughout his career but struggled against equally skilled wrestler, who were much bigger. Had Beell been five inches taller and close to two hundred pounds, he would have been in the same class of wrestler as Frank Gotch and Tom Jenkins.

The men met in a two-out-of-three falls match at the Old Arsenal on Broadway.[lxxxii] Beell started the match aggressively and it cost him.

Beell dove for Zbyszko's leg to secure a single leg takedown. Zbyszko stepped back to avoid the dive causing Beell to fall on his hands and knees in front of Zbyszko.[lxxxiii]

Zbyszko dropped onto Beell's upper back as he put a half-Nelson on the prone Beell. Zbyszko flipped Beell to his back and pressed his full weight on the chest of the helpless Beell. Zbyszko won the first fall in one minute, nineteen seconds.[lxxxiv] A shocked Beell tried to regroup during the twenty-minute intermission.

Beell put on a much stronger performance in the second fall. Zbyszko attempted to gain single and double leg takedowns, but Beell sprawled defensively each time. Beell caught Zbyszko in a front face lock. Beell used it to wrench Zbyszko's neck and grind his face.[lxxxv] Beell's offense irritated Zbyszko more than it hurt him.

At the forty-five-minute mark, Zbyszko spun to Beell's back and was behind him. Beell reached up with one arm, trapped Zbyszko's head and intended to throw Zbyszko over his shoulder with a flying mare, while Beell kneeled on the mat.[lxxxvi]

Before Beell could execute the throw, Zbyszko applied a reverse Nelson and flipped Beell to his back on the mat. Zbyszko pressed his weight down on Beell's chest. Beell bridged for a full two minutes but he could not prevent the inevitable. Zbyszko pinned Bell at 51 minutes for the second fall and match.[lxxxvii]

Zbyszko expressed great delight at beating Beell, who won the American Heavyweight Wrestling Championship from Frank Gotch in December 1906. Zbyszko was not aware, nor was the public, that Gotch and Beell worked those title matches in December 1906.

On January 6, 1910, Zbyszko defeated frequent Gotch foe, Tom Jenkins, in two straight falls.[lxxxviii] Jenkins wrestled sparingly since accepting the self-defense instructor position at West

Point. Zbyszko's victory would have been more impressive five years earlier.

On January 10, 1910, Zbyszko wrestled Charles "Kid" Cutler in Chicago, Illinois. Cutler won the American Heavyweight Wrestling Championship in 1911. He held the title at least three times between 1911 and 1915.[lxxxix]

Cutler represented a step up in competitions for Zbyszko. Since the men were close in skill level, the match unfolded as most legitimate contests did at the time. The wrestlers stalemated for extended periods of time with little action before one of the wrestlers scored a fall.

Figure 11- Charles "Kid" Cutler (Public Domain)

The men wrestled at Chicago's Coliseum. It took Zbyszko 51 minutes, 57 seconds to secure a chancery and bar arm hold to take the first fall. Zbyszko used the same hold to defeat the visibly fatigued Cutler at 15 minutes, 59 seconds.[xc]

On January 18th, Zbyszko was back in Buffalo, New York to slam the giant Frenchman, Raouel de Rouen. The reporter covering the match said "the greatest crowd that ever witnessed a wrestling bout in this city" turned out to watch the match.[xci] Unfortunately, the reporter did not record the actual fan attendance or gate.

Referee W. J. Kelly disqualified de Rouen for the first fall at the 28-minute mark.[xcii] Each time Zbyszko grabbed de Rouen, de Rouen grabbed the ring ropes to prevent Zbyszko's throws. Grabbing the ropes to prevent a throw or hold was a foul at the time.

Kelly warned de Rouen repeatedly to stop grabbing the ropes. Finally, a frustrated Kelly disqualified de Rouen.

De Rouen regretted not using the same tactics during the second fall. Zbyszko lifted de Rouen high off the mat and slammed him forcefully on his head and shoulders. The slam knocked de Rouen senseless. Zbyszko easily pinned him. Kelly raised Zbyszko's arm. It took him 28 minutes to win the second fall and match.[xciii]

On January 21st, Zbyszko was in Toledo, Ohio to wrestle English wrestler, James Paar. Zbyszko used a scissors hold to pin Parr for the first fall in 26 minutes. It took Zbyszko only 12 minutes to take the second fall and match with an armlock.[xciv]

On February 3, 1910, Zbyszko avenged an earlier defeat, when he wrestled Henry Ordeman, the winner of their handicap match. During his tour leading up to the Gotch match, no one defeated Zbyszko. However, he did lose handicapped matches where he agreed to throw his opponent so many times within a specified period.

Herman booked the rematch between Zbyszko and Ordeman in Minneapolis, Minnesota.[xcv] The setting made sense as Ordeman was based in Minneapolis. Matching Zbyszko against a strong, local favorite usually led to a large paying crowd.

Ordeman proved a tough opponent. Although Zbyszko outweighed him by forty pounds, Ordeman stifled Zbyszko's offense for over an hour. Zbyszko pinned Ordeman with a crotch hold and half-Nelson after 1 hour, 23 minutes and 10 seconds of hard wrestling.[xcvi]

Ordeman visibly weakened after sixty minutes but Zbyszko showed no signs of tiring. The twenty-minute intermission provided Ordeman a second wind. Zbyszko finally secured another crotch hold and half-Nelson combination to pin Ordeman at 43 minutes, 30 seconds.[xcvii]

Zbyszko won the rematch in two straight falls, but he had to work for it. Zbyszko took the next match only for the money.

12,000 fans turned out to see Zbyszko wrestle Yussif Mahmout, the man Gotch easily defeated early in 1909.[xcviii] Zbyszko knew Mahmout, a Bulgarian, well from their time in Europe. Zbyszko despised Mahmout.

Like Gotch, Mahmout had no compunction about fouling his opponent, if it helped him win a bout. Zbyszko defeated Mahmout in Europe and was unimpressed with Mahmout's tactics.

Georg Hackenschmidt shared Zbyszko's opinion of Mahmout. When he returned to the United States in 1911 for the Gotch rematch, Gotch wanted Hackenschmidt to wrestle Mahmout to prove he was worthy of a rematch. Hackenschmidt told Gotch to go pound salt. Gotch relented. Hackenschmidt wrestled Zbyszko instead.[xcix]

Figure 12- Yussif Mahmout around 1910 (Public Domain)

Zbyszko agreed to wrestle Mahmout but stipulated that Mahmout had to throw him twice within sixty minutes or the referee would award the match to Zbyszko.

For this match, Zbyszko weighed 250 pounds. Mahmout weighed 208 pounds. Both men used their weight and strength to push and bang into each other like a couple of bulls for the first thirty minutes.[c]

As Mahmout entered the ring, he was visibly suffering with three boils on his right arm. The affliction rendered his right arm almost useless. During the match, Mahmout let his right arm hang when he did not need to use it. He used the arm when he needed to, but he could not hide the grimace every time he did so.[ci]

At the 34-minute mark, Mahmout secured a single leg takedown and took Zbyszko to the mat. Zbyszko pulled his leg loose and stood back up.[cii] Knowing he only needed to keep Mahmout from throwing him, Zbyszko wrestled defensively for the first forty-five minutes of the match.

At the forty-five-minute mark, Zbyszko spun to Mahmout's back. He applied a wristlock to submit Mahmout. Mahmout escaped but Zbyszko moved to toehold. Mahmout kicked like a mule to escape. Mahmout scrambled back to his feet.[ciii]

Zbyszko wrestled defensively after this offensive flurry. The referee raised his hand at the sixty-minute mark. Zbyszko won a $1,000 purse plus a $500 side bet from Mahmout.[civ] Their managers started negotiating for a rematch after Mahmout's arm healed.

While the tour started off with a couple stumbles, Zbyszko regrouped well in January and February 1910. Could he keep the momentum going over the next three months leading to his championship match with Frank Gotch?

Figure 13-Stanislaus Zbyszko from the St. Louis Post-Dispatch in 1910 (Public Domain)

Chapter 4 – Zbyszko's Tour Continues

While Zbyszko continued touring, Chicago promoters collaborated with Jack Herman and Emil Klank, the manager for both Gotch and Mahmout. They were determined to secure a rematch between Zbyszko and Mahmout. Herman agreed to a two-out-of-three fall match between the men contested for a $9,000 purse.[cv] Mahmout did not agree at first.

Zbyszko demanded a purse split of 80 percent to him and 20 percent to Mahmout. Mahmout refused. They were stuck at an impasse until Zbyszko accepted a purse split of 75 percent to him and 25 percent to Mahmout. Klank and Mahmout reluctantly agreed.[cvi] The purse split proved promoters expected Zbyszko to draw the crowd.

On March 22, 1910, Zbyszko wrestled perennial contender, Dr. Benjamin Roller. Zbyszko and Roller pulled and tugged at each other for 2 hours, 17 minutes without either scoring a fall. The Kansas City Police stopped the match for curfew. Referee Dave Porteus declared the match a draw.[cvii]

Dr. Roller pushed the pace for the first hour, but he tired during the second hour. Zbyszko took over and was dominating the match when the police stopped it. Ringside reporters disagreed on whether Zbyszko would have won the match if the police allowed it to continue.[cviii]

Zbyszko wrestled a local wrestler in Buffalo on Friday, March 25, 1910. Harry Davis avoided Zbyszko for five minutes. Zbyszko finally grabbed Davis in a body hold and lifted him off the ground.[cix]

Zbyszko slammed Davis to the mat but unbeknownst to Zbyszko the mat was thin where he slammed Davis. The impact knocked Davis out. Davis' body went completely limp.[cx]

It took two doctors over ten minutes to revive Davis. Zbyszko admitted to reporters that he thought he killed Davis. Zbyszko stated his intention to take it a little easier on lesser competition in the future.[cxi]

On March 30th, Zbyszko met Yussif Mahmout for a rematch in Chicago at the Empire Club. Promoters claimed the winner of the bout would face Frank Gotch in Chicago for the World Title.[cxii]

However, Gotch already agreed to wrestle Zbyszko after their draw in November 1909. Promoters often used such claims to publicize a match between wrestlers.

Zbyszko defeated Mahmout in two straight falls. Mahmout wrestled offensively throughout the match. Zbyszko bided his time and made Mahmout pay for his mistakes. Zbyszko applied a crotch hold and half-Nelson to score the first fall in 1 hour, 4 minutes and 51 seconds.[cxiii]

After 25 minutes, 43 seconds, Zbyszko threw Mahmout with a back arm and half-Nelson for the second fall and match.[cxiv] Zbyszko enjoyed the decisive victory over his hated rival.

On April 1, 1910, the *Wilkes-Barre Times Leader* reported Emil Klank, Gotch's manager, and Jack Herman, Zbyszko's manager, may not reach agreement on a match.[cxv] Gotch demanded sixty percent of the gate for the proposed title match in Chicago. Gotch said he was tired of drawing big gates in America for foreign wrestlers.[cxvi]

Zbyszko flatly refused any agreement other than a fifty-fifty split of the gate.[cxvii] Fans waited to see which wrestler blinked first but a title match was still likely. Too much money was on the line for the men not to come to an agreement.

Gotch further put the screws to Zbyszko by demanding that he beat Dr. Benjamin Roller before Gotch wrestled him. He reiterated that he would only wrestle Zbyszko for sixty percent of the gate, whether Gotch won, lost, or drew with Zbyszko.[cxviii]

On April 21st, Zbyszko wrestled Yankee Rogers at the Ninth Regiment Armory in Wilkes-Barre, Pennsylvania. 3,000 fans turned out to see the top contender for Gotch's title.[cxix]

Zbyszko needed only thirty-five minutes to throw Rogers with a head hold and chancery. Zbyszko won the second fall and match by pinning Rogers with a bar arm and half-Nelson.[cxx]

On April 26th, Zbyszko wrestled Mort Henderson, billed as the Champion of the Northwest but more famous as the Masked Marvel during the 1915 International Wrestling Tournament.[cxxi] 5,000 fans, mostly from Polish Society in New York, crowded into Grand Central Palace.[cxxii] They came to see Zbyszko as they wildly cheered him throughout the match.

Figure 14- Mort Henderson circa 1915 (Public Domain)

Zbyszko needed only four minutes, thirty seconds to pin Henderson with a right arm lock and wheel hold. Henderson did better in the second fall. It took Zbyszko twenty minutes, 30 seconds to win the second fall and match with his favorite crotch hold and half-Nelson combination.[cxxiii]

On April 29th, Zbyszko travelled back to Chicago to wrestle Dr. Benjamin Roller, one of Gotch's demands to secure a title shot. However, Dr. Roller performed an emergency surgery in Seattle, so he was unable to travel. Jess Westergaard, who stalemated Zbyszko in December 1909 under his real name Jess Reimers, substituted for Dr. Roller.[cxxiv]

Zbyszko wrestled Westergaard for 51 minutes before he secured Gotch's pet hold, the toehold, on Westergaard. Zbyszko wrenched Westergaard's leg hard causing Westergaard to yell out.[cxxv]

The referee requested a doctor look at the leg. He diagnosed a ligament injury and recommended the referee stop the match. The referee raised Zbyszko's hand, but Zbyszko refused the victory. He wanted to defeat Westergaard but not injure him.[cxxvi]

Emil Klank and Jack Herman entered into an agreement for a championship match on Decoration Day (Memorial Day) 1910. Decoration Day was May 30th in 1910 but the men wrestled on June 1, 1910.[cxxvii]

The Empire Club promoted the wrestling card. They scheduled the card for Comiskey Park, the home of the Chicago White Sox. Before the negotiations concluded, Klank and the Empire Club ripped off Stanislaus Zbyszko.

Gotch now demanded sixty-five percent of the gate. The Empire Club wanted thirty-five percent leaving Zbyszko only five percent of the gate. Herman yelled robbery but the other parties refused to back down. He had no choice but to accept the pitiful purse.[cxxviii]

Herman was confident that Zbyszko could defeat Gotch. Herman reasoned that Zbyszko's future earnings justified this slight. It was only the first slight in dealing with Gotch and his team.

In what reporters originally identified as his last match before wrestling Gotch, Zbyszko wrestled Raoul de Rouen in Detroit on May 4th. Promoters scheduled Zbyszko to wrestle both de Rouen and Charles Cutler. The attendance was so poor, promoters notified the wrestlers and the crowd that they only had enough cash to pay Zbyszko and one opponent.[cxxix]

Cutler lost the coin toss, so Zbyszko wrestled de Rouen. Zbyszko agreed to throw de Rouen twice in an hour.[cxxx]

De Rouen's offense consisted of frequent palm strikes and even biting. Detroit Police Captain Baker jumped into the ring at one point and told the referee and de Rouen that he would stop the match if de Rouen did not stop biting immediately.[cxxxi]

De Rouen's cheating did not help much. Zbyszko pinned him with a scissors hold for the first fall after only twenty minutes. Zbyszko used his favorite combination of the crotch hold and half-Nelson to take the second fall and match after nine minutes, thirty seconds.[cxxxii] De Rouen never troubled Zbyszko in this bout.

As they approached the match with Gotch, Herman and Zbyszko threw the Empire Club into confusion by demanding a Polish American referee.[cxxxiii] Still smarting from the Gotch team's financial maneuvering, they demanded a referee other than Ed Smith, the usual referee for Gotch's big Chicago bouts.

The posturing went on for three weeks before the parties agreed to Dick Fleming, the regular referee for Empire Club wrestling cards.[cxxxiv] Due to Gotch's frequent fouling in big matches, Herman and Zbyszko showed wisdom in worrying about the referee. Time would tell if Fleming was an improvement over Ed Smith, who allowed Gotch to foul freely.

On May 16, 1910, Zbyszko met one of Gotch's original demands even though they already agreed to the Chicago bout. Zbyszko wrestled Dr. Benjamin Roller in a finish match at Buffalo, New York.[cxxxv]

Zbyszko and Roller stalemated each other for an hour until Zbyszko lifted Roller overhead with a body hold. Zbyszko had one arm trapped against Roller's body when Zbyszko slammed Roller to the mat for the first fall in one hour, five minutes and forty seconds.[cxxxvi]

Roller rolled on the mat in pain. His seconds entered the ring and helped him to the dressing room. The doctor diagnosed a separated shoulder. Against the doctor's advice, Roller insisted on returning for the second fall. He walked to the ring with his arm hanging at his side.[cxxxvii]

At the start of the second fall, Zbyszko immediately spun to

Roller's back. He started to turn Roller to the mat, but his seconds threw in a sponge signifying they were stopping the contest. Zbyszko won the second fall and match in one minute, forty seconds.[cxxxviii] Gotch did not have any right to demand Zbyszko defeat Dr. Roller, but Zbyszko met the condition anyway.

Figure 15- Dr. Benjamin F. Roller (Public Domain)

Everything looked good for the match until Chicago Mayor Fred A. Busse refused to issue a permit for the match on Decoration Day (Memorial Day). Busse said he wanted the day preserved for remembering service members killed in the line of duty. He worried fans would attend the wrestling matches instead of decorating the graves of the fallen.[cxxxix]

The promoters faced serious monetary loss with this decision. Gotch and Zbyszko could demand the $2,000 forfeit if the match did not go on as scheduled. Charles Comiskey could also demand a day of rent for Comiskey Park, the site of the match.[cxl] The promoters reluctantly sued the city.

The city lost the first round in court. Since the city allowed amusement parks, beer gardens, theaters, and tracks to operate on Memorial Day, the court saw Mayor Busse's conduct as prejudicial against professional wrestling.[cxli] The Empire Club asked the judge to delay any decision so they could speak with the Mayor's Office about a compromise.

The Mayor's Office refused to compromise. The judge issued a writ demanding the mayor issue a permit, but the mayor could appeal the decision. The Mayor's Office did appeal with the intent of delaying the case until after May 30th making the permit issue moot.[cxlii]

The Empire Club relented. After speaking with Gotch's and Zbyszko's camps, they moved the match to the Chicago Coliseum. They also postponed the match for two days until Wednesday, June 1, 1910.[cxliii]

With the match moved back two days, Zbyszko decided to accept one more booking before the match with Gotch. Zbyszko wrestled well-regarded light heavyweight Charley Olson in St. Louis, Missouri on Sunday, March 29, 1910.[cxliv]

Zbyszko told reporters he weighed 245 pounds for this match. Zbyszko impressed fans and reporters with his great strength. He pulled out of all Olsen's hold attempts.[cxlv]

Zbyszko applied a back lock and scissors hold for the first fall in twenty-eight minutes. It took Zbyszko sixteen more minutes to win the second fall with an arm hold and roll.[cxlvi]

Zbyszko had trained hard and dominated his recent competition. He felt good going into the match with Frank Gotch. He was as ready as possible to beat the World Champion.

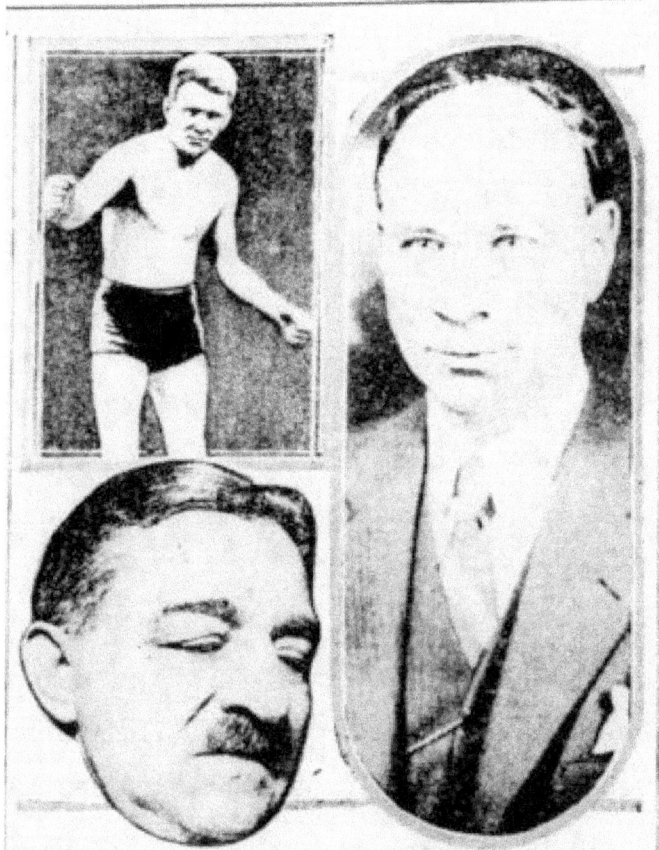

Figure 16-Charley Olson is in the upper left corner (Public Domain)

Chapter 5 – World Title Match

Zbyszko actively toured leading up to his title challenge of Frank Gotch. Gotch barely wrestled outside of the training room. In fact, he wrestled two professional matches prior to wrestling Zbyszko in June. After wrestling Zbyszko in Chicago, Gotch did not compete again in 1910.

On February 28, 1910, Gotch arrived in Chicago, Illinois to wrestle Jim Esson of Aberdeen, Scotland. 4,000 fans paid to see the main event at the Chicago Coliseum.[cxlvii]

The reporter for the *Chicago Tribune* reminded readers that 4,000 fans for a championship match was a small crowd. The Empire Club, promoter for the upcoming title match, promoted this disappointing card.^{cxlviii}

Gotch worked quickly on this night. After Referee Fleming started the match, Gotch took Esson down to the mat. As Esson tried to break loose, Gotch worked for a toehold. It took him ten minutes, but he secured his pet hold on the challenger. Esson submitted immediately. Gotch won the first fall in 11 minutes, 25 seconds.^{cxlix}

During the ten-minute intermission, Gotch decided to make the match more of a workout for him. He told his trainer, Martin "Farmer" Burns, that he would not use the toehold in the second fall.

Gotch remained on the offensive. He took Esson to the mat three times with a single leg takedown. Each time, Esson squirmed away and returned to his feet.^{cl}

After Esson escaped a third time, Gotch applied a crotch hold and chancery. Esson tried to escape but Gotch flipped him to his back. Fleming signaled the pinfall at 13 minutes, 23 seconds. Gotch won the match in two straight falls.[cli]

Gotch's dominance hurt Esson's ability to draw a crowd after this match. Promoters had signed Esson for a series of ten matches.[clii] They had a tough time drawing crowds over the next nine matches after this crushing loss.

On May 13, 1910, Gotch traveled to Calumet, Michigan to wrestle Chris Person, a skilled wrestler from Duluth, Minnesota.[cliii]

Gotch agreed to throw Person twice in an hour or forfeit the match. The men wrestled at the Amphridome in Calumet, Michigan.[cliv]

Gotch played with Person in the same way he toyed with Jimmy Esson. Gotch secured the crotch hold and half-Nelson combination on Person four or five times. While Gotch started to turn Person, Person squirmed out of the hold.[clv]

Gotch dropped to his hands and knees to allow Person to apply holds on him. Gotch broke the four or five holds to laughs from the crowd.[clvi]

After this show of superiority, Gotch lifted Person up with the crotch hold and dumped him on the mat. Gotch flipped Person to his back with a half-Nelson to pin him for the first fall at 21 minutes, 15 seconds.[clvii]

After the ten-minute intermission, Gotch needed only 10 minutes, 50 seconds to flip Person to the mat with a reverse waist hold.[clviii] Person's shoulders hit the mat for the second fall and match. Gotch dominated another opponent.

Gotch surprised the Empire Club when he declined to setup a training camp in Chicago. Gotch trained in his hometown of Humboldt, Iowa. Since the summer of 1909, Gotch spent more time in Humboldt and less time on the road. He traveled to Chicago for the match on May 31, 1910

8,000 fans crowded into the Chicago Coliseum for the big title match on June 2, 1910.[clix] Two hours before the doors opened, the crowd blocked traffic on Wabash Avenue.

Figure 17- Gotch Takes Zbyszko's Back in the Match (Public Domain)

Zbyszko entered the ring first at 10:00 p.m. Gotch quickly followed. Referee Dick Fleming gave the men instructions at center ring, sent them to their corners and started the match.clx

Gotch and Zbyszko walked to the center of the ring for the customary handshake. After the handshake, the wrestlers normally took two or three steps back or returned to their corners and then move towards each other to tie up. Frank Gotch had other plans.

As soon as Zbyszko offered his hand to shake, Gotch touched Zbyszko's hand instead of shaking it and tackled Zbyszko to the mat. As a shocked Zbyszko looked at him, Gotch flipped Zbyszko to his back with a bar arm and half-Nelson combination. Referee Fleming tapped Gotch on the back signaling he won the first fall in six seconds.[clxi]

Zbyszko and his manager Jack Herman exploded over Gotch's dirty trick. They demanded Fleming restart the match and disallow the pin. Fleming stated he started the match. While the handshake was customary, it was not necessary. Zbyszko needed to guard against an attack once the bell rang.[clxii]

Figure 18-Artist Rendering of the First Fall from the Chicago Tribune, June 2, 1910 (Public Domain)

Zbyszko left the ring for the ten-minute intermission. He told the Empire Club representatives that he was leaving if they did not reverse the referee's ruling on Gotch's poor sportsmanship.[clxiii]

Zbyszko's ultimatum put the Empire Club in a tough position. As promoters, they did not have the power to reverse the referee's decision. They also had a full house of 8,000 fans who would not be happy if Zbyszko just left after the first fall. Crowds rioted for less.

The promoters begged Zbyszko to continue the match. They reminded him that he could still win the next two falls to take the championship from Gotch. If he walked out, Gotch may never agree to wrestle him again.[clxiv]

Herman saw the wisdom in this reasoning and convinced Zbyszko to continue the match. Gotch's tactics shook Zbyszko up though. He wrestled defensively in the second fall because if he made a mistake, Gotch could take the second fall and end the match.

Despite Gotch's deplorable conduct in the first fall, the newspaper reporters covering the bout portrayed Zbyszko as a fool for falling for Gotch's dirty trick.[clxv] They would not have covered it the same way if Zbyszko tackled Gotch during the handshake. The reporters would condemn Gotch's tactic for the disgraceful conduct it was.

At the start of the second fall, Gotch pushed Zbyszko around the ring. Since Zbyszko held a strength advantage, Gotch's tactics were a little surprising. Gotch adopted a higher percentage attack by grabbing a single leg takedown.[clxvi]

Gotch dumped Zbyszko to the mat, but Zbyszko scrambled back to his feet. Gotch dove for and finished two more single leg takedowns, but each time Zbyszko scrambled back to his feet.[clxvii]

Gotch dove into a double leg takedown and took Zbyszko back to the mat. Gotch made a rare mistake on the mat. He went for a half-Nelson but missed his hold. Zbyszko spun to Gotch's back for his first offense of the second fall.clxviii

Zbyszko secured a waist hold but before he could turn Gotch, Gotch stood up as he broke Zbyszko's grip around his waist.clxix Zbyszko showed renewed energy as he grabbed a single leg takedown and took Gotch back to the mat.

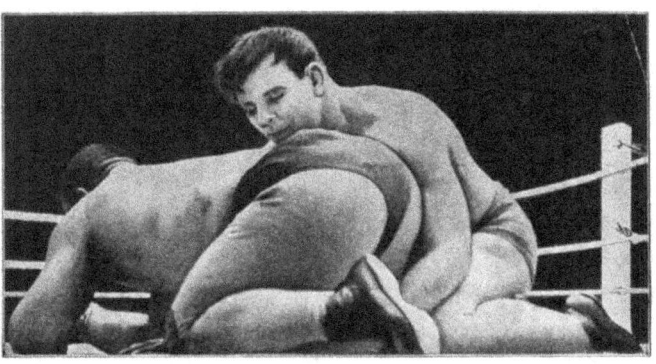

Figure 19- Gotch Working for Toehold on Zbyszko (Public Domain)

Gotch escaped again and forced Zbyszko down to all fours. Gotch tried for two toeholds, but Zbyszko avoided both. However, Gotch applied a hammerlock. Zbyszko rolled out of the hold to stop Gotch from wrenching his shoulder.[clxx]

Zbyszko fought for another waist hold, which Gotch countered by sitting on the mat. Gotch tried to scramble to his feet, but Zbyszko brought him back to the mat.[clxxi]

While sitting on the mat, Gotch broke Zbyszko's grip and spun behind him. Zbyszko tried to stand up, but Gotch already had his foot. Gotch cranked on a toehold.[clxxii]

Zbyszko yanked and pulled with his leg. Gotch held on for five to ten seconds before Zbyszko broke free.[clxxiii] It was long enough to hurt Zbyszko.

Zbyszko backed into a corner and reached down to check on his ankle. Gotch pounced on the opening. He rushed into the corner, secured a bear hug under Zbyszko's arm, and dumped him to the mat.[clxxiv]

Gotch followed Zbyszko to the mat. Gotch applied a bar arm and wristlock combination, flipping Zbyszko to his back and pinning him for the second fall and match at 27 minutes, 33 seconds.[clxxv]

Zbyszko left ringside and did not speak with reporters. Frank Gotch, Jack Herman, and referee Dick Fleming did make statements. As expected, the controversy over the first fall took center stage.

Gotch and Fleming stated the first fall was clean. Herman questioned the first fall but allowed that Gotch may have scored within the rules. Herman said he warned Zbyszko to be on the lookout for dirty tricks, but Gotch still caught him unaware.[clxxvi]

Herman agreed with Gotch that Zbyszko's lack of catch-as-catch-can training hurt him in this match. Zbyszko wrestled Greco-Roman wrestling matches until he came to the United States.[clxxvii]

After this match, Zbyszko decided to continue campaigning in the United States and acquire the necessary experience in catch wrestling to challenge Frank Gotch again. Frank Gotch had other plans.

Figure 20- Artist Rendering of Frank Gotch hugging the $23,000 purse he won in the Zbyszko match from the Chicago Tribune, June 2, 1910 (Public Domain)

Chapter 6 – Gotch Wants One More Pay Day

The most important event affecting the future of Frank Gotch's career occurred on January 11, 1911. Gotch married the former Gladys Oestrich at her parent's home in Humboldt, Iowa.

Mrs. Gotch preferred that Frank retire from the ring which he had been hinting at since he defeated Hackenschmidt for the world championship in 1908.

Gotch told Gladys he was retiring prior to their engagement but a potential big money rematch with Georg Hackenschmidt in 1911 changed his mind.[clxxviii] Klank had been trying to lure Hackenschmidt back to the United States for a rematch since 1908. Hackenschmidt refused until late in 1910.

Hackenschmidt dealt with chronic knee injury since the time of the 1908 match. It hindered his training. Hackenschmidt trained other wrestlers but did not wrestle professionally in 1909 and 1910. In 1910, Hackenschmidt started to feel like he could train enough to regain his world class conditioning and wrestling skills.

Gotch returning to the ring surprised Gladys. She told newspaper reporters that Frank told her he was retiring and had not informed her he changed his mind.[clxxix]

The reporter asked Gladys if she would end the engagement if Gotch wrestled professionally again. "No, I would not want to say that, but I cannot say definitely until I talk things over with him.

He promised me - but I guess I'd better see Frank."clxxx

Gladys Gotch accepted Frank Gotch wrestling for another two years, but she preferred he stay home. Galdys' wishes weighed on Frank Gotch and affected how willing he was to train and wrestle in the twilight of his career.

Figure 21- Gladys Gotch from the Evansville Press, January 7, 1911 (Public Domain)

Gotch getting married was big news. Newspapers throughout the country carried coverage of the wedding. Gotch was 33 years old and turned thirty-four on April 27th. Gladys turned twenty a week before her wedding, but she exhibited more maturity than the average twenty-year-old.[clxxxi]

Right after their marriage on January 11, 1911, in Humboldt, Frank and Gladys Gotch traveled to Chicago, Illinois. A vaudeville circuit engaged Gotch to perform on stage.[clxxxii]

I wrote extensively about Gotch's wrestling and training during 1911 in *Gotch vs. Hackenschmidt*. I will briefly touch on topics important to this book but would point readers, who want to gain an extensive understanding of the big match between Gotch and

Hackenschmidt, to *Gotch vs. Hackenschmidt*.

Gotch showed foresight in coming back for one more big pay day. The rematch with Hackenschmidt drew over 30,000 fans and a huge gate for Gotch.[clxxxiii] A wrestling match did not draw over 30,000 fans again until the 1930s.

Prior to his September 4th match with Hackenschmidt, Gotch did not wrestle one competitive match leading up to the match. Gotch worked matches with other trainees of "Farmer" Burns.

On March 25, 1911, Gotch wrestled Tom Jenkins in a contest, but Jenkins was well past his prime. The men met in Denver, Colorado, where Gotch defeated Jenkins in two straight falls. Gotch used a crotch hold and half-Nelson to win two straight falls in less than thirty minutes.[clxxxiv]

Gotch worked his matches in 1912 as well. In fact, after wrestling Hackenschmidt, Gotch wrestled one more contest in his career.

Gotch wrestled another foreign wrestler in the final match of his career. However, Gotch refused to wrestle one foreign wrestler no matter how hard he tried to secure a rematch.

Figure 22- Frank Gotch Caricature from 1911 (Public Domain)

Chapter 7 – Zbyszko Presses for Rematch

After losing to Gotch, Stanislaus Zbyszko returned to Poland for the summer to consider his next steps. Zbyszko decided to return to the United States at the end of October 1910 to campaign for a rematch with Gotch.[clxxxv]

Herman told Zbyszko upon his return that Frank Gotch retired and was marrying in early 1911.[clxxxvi] Momentarily thwarted in his efforts to rematch Gotch, Herman and Zbyszko looked for a way to claim the vacant world title.

Zbyszko signed to meet Dr. Benjamin Roller in Pittsburgh on November 9, 1910, in a match to claim the world title.[clxxxvii] Gotch nixed these plans when he announced his return at the end of December 1910.

Oddly, Zbyszko and Roller agreed to meet in a Greco-Roman wrestling match, which were rare in the United States. Even without Gotch returning, it was not a certainty than fans would accept Zbyszko as Gotch's successor based on Zbyszko defeating Roller in Zbyszko's specialty.

Zbyszko had not given up on improving his catch wrestling skills. While he returned to Poland, Zbyszko paid three American catch wrestlers to travel with him. Zbyszko trained with the three men for the four months he in Poland to quickly improve his catch wrestling skills.[clxxxviii]

Since he and Dr. Roller wrestled in the Greco-Roman wrestling style, Zbyszko agreed to throw Roller twice within the sixty-minute time limit or forfeit the match to Roller.[clxxxix] Zbyszko made a mistake in agreeing to this stipulation.

Zbyszko and Roller wrestled hard for fifty minutes until Zbyszko called the match to an end. He admitted he could not throw Roller twice in the last ten minutes, so he conceded the bout to Roller.[cxc]

To make his case to the American wrestling fans for a rematch with Gotch, Zbyszko needed to score impressive victories and show improvement in catch wrestling. Zbyszko took a step forward in his next match.

On December 2, 1910, Zbyszko wrestled another handicap match at the Grand Central Palace in New York City. Zbyszko wrestled Andrew Kidriat and former American

Heavyweight Wrestling Champion Tom Jenkins.[cxci]

Zbyszko threw Kidriat in 10 minutes, 38 seconds. It took Zbyszko a little longer to throw Jenkins. He needed 15 minutes, 40 seconds to throw the old champion.[cxcii]

On December 14th, Zbyszko wrestled his last match in 1910. In front of 1,500 fans at Bridgeport, Connecticut's Eagle Hall, Zbyszko wrestled Swedish strongman and wrestler Hjamlar Lundin.[cxciii]

Controversy broke out before the match because Zbyszko showed up in short trunks and bare foot. Lundin claimed that Zbyszko agreed to wear long tights and shoes for the match.[cxciv]

Figure 23-Hjamlar Lundin in 1913 (Public Domain)

Zbyszko's manager Jack Herman agreed with Lundin that Zbyszko agreed to wear shoes. However, Zbyszko forgot them because he normally wrestled barefoot in Europe and his early United States matches. Herman said that Zbyszko did not agree to wear long tights.[cxcv]

Zbyszko agreed to wear wrestling shoes if Lundin's team could find shoes in Zbyszko's size. Lundin's team asked around, but they did not find a suitable pair. Lundin begrudgingly allowed Zbyszko to wrestle barefoot.[cxcvi]

The men wrestled 2-out-of-3 falls with falls awarded by pin only. The men wrestled in the catch wrestling style.[cxcvii]

Lundin was taller but Zbyszko had the weight advantage. Zbyszko knew he was stronger and showed his power to great advantage. Zbyszko allowed Lundin to apply holds on him only to power out of each attempt.[cxcviii]

Zbyszko only faced danger once in the match when he rushed in, grabbed Lundin in a head chancery and attempted to throw Lundin over his shoulder. Due to heavy perspiration from both men, Lundin's head slipped out of Zbyszko's grip and Zbyszko fell on his butt.[cxcix]

Lundin tried to turn Zbyszko, but he stood up and broke Lundin's grip from around his waist. He looked sheepishly at the crowd acknowledging his mistake.[cc]

At the 35-minute mark, Zbyszko used a half-Nelson and crotch hold to turn Lundin's shoulders to the mat for the first fall at 35 minutes, 15 seconds.[cci] The men retired to their dressing rooms for the intermission.

Figure 24- Stanislaus Zbyszko Wrestling in 1910. In this picture, he is wearing shoes, but he often wrestled barefoot.

Lundin looked exhausted but Zbyszko appeared fresh coming out of the intermission. Zbyszko decided to press the attack on his tiring opponent.

Zbyszko took Lundin to the mat. He used a scissors hold and half-Nelson to win the match in two straight falls. Zbyszko pinned Lundin for the second fall in seven minutes.[ccii]

Before taking a month off for the holidays, Zbyszko agreed to wrestle South African wrestler Peter Nogert on January 11, 1911.

Zbyszko spent the holidays in Buffalo, New York with his manager Jack Herman. Since he was already in town, Zbyszko accepted a tune-up match on January 2, 1911, in Buffalo.[cciii]

Swiss wrestler John Lemm challenged Zbyszko in a two-out-of-three falls match. Lemm surprised Zbyszko by lifting him off the ground but Lemm lost his balance and fell backwards with Zbyszko on top of him. Zbyszko fell into the pin scoring the first fall on Lemm in one minute, thirty seconds.[cciv]

Lemm injured his chest or shoulders in the fall but insisted on continuing the match. He tied up with Zbyszko but was helpless to resist. Zbyszko released Lemm and refused to wrestle him in his feeble condition. After speaking with Lemm, the referee awarded Zbyszko the match in two straight falls.[ccv]

On January 11th, Zbyszko traveled back to Bridgeport, Connecticut for his match with Peter "The Giant" Nogert. Nogert, at 245 pounds, enjoyed a five-pound weight advantage over Zbyszko.[ccvi] Like Zbyszko's other opponents, Nogert towered over Zbyszko. Zbyszko rarely enjoyed a height advantage.

The men wrestled at the Eagles Hall. Professor James Atlas promoted the card and refereed the main event. Fans crowded into the Eagles Hall to see the match.[ccvii]

Zbyszko won the first fall after 45 minutes by using a hammerlock to roll Nogert to his back.[ccviii] The hammerlock puts tremendous pressure on the rotor cuff in the shoulder of the arm the wrestler is applying the hold.

The men kept up a solid pace in the second fall until Nogert fell or Zbyszko pushed him off the raised platform on which they were wrestling. As he fell four feet from the platform, Nogert's side struck the ringside table. The collision broke one of Nogert's ribs causing him to concede the second fall to Zbyszko.[ccix]

The fans hissed at the decision, but Professor Atlas cleared Zbyszko of a deliberate foul. After telling the audience no foul occurred, Atlas raised Zbyszko's hand in victory. Zbyszko won the second fall in eleven minutes.[ccx]

Zbyszko experienced a rough patch at the end of January 1911. On January 23rd, Zbyszko wrestled Gotch protégé, Henry Ordeman at the Light Guard Armory in Detroit, Michigan.[ccxi]

Zbyszko agreed to throw Ordeman twice in ninety minutes. While knowledgeable observers saw the extra thirty minutes as an advantage for Zbyszko, Zbyszko did not throw Ordeman once. The crowd cheered Ordeman's effort. Despite his spotty record in handicap matches, Zbyszko continued accepting these stipulations in his matches.[ccxii]

On January 27, 1911, Zbyszko wrestled Nogert again along with Andrew Kandrat. Zbyszko needed to throw both men in an hour or concede the match.[ccxiii]

Zbyszko threw Nogert, who had recovered from his rib injury, in 42 minutes, 58 seconds. Zbyszko could not throw Kandrat and conceded the match to his opponents.[ccxiv]

In February 1911, Frank Gotch's manager Emil Klank offered to setup a tournament between the men he considered the top contenders for a title shot with Gotch: Zbyszko, Georg Hackenschmidt and Yussif Mahmout.[ccxv]

Hackenschmidt ruined this plan when he categorically refused to wrestle Mahmout. He knew Mahmout from Europe, considered him a dirty wrestler, and refused to wrestle him. Hackenschmidt state he would be happy to wrestle Zbyszko, who he considered a gentleman.[ccxvi]

On February 9, 1911, Hackenschmidt wrestled Zbyszko at Madison Square Garden for the opportunity to wrestle Frank Gotch for the world title. Hackenschmidt agreed to throw Zbyszko twice in ninety minutes.[ccxvii]

Hackenschmidt weighed 210 pounds compared to 250 pounds for Zbyszko. Hackenschmidt twice threw Zbyszko over his shoulder. Zbyszko hit hard but rolled to his feet without a pin each time.[ccxviii]

Zbyszko tried to put Gotch's toehold on Hackenschmidt twice, but Hackenschmidt broke it by turning a back somersault both times. The men also stalemated each other for prolonged periods.^{ccxix}

Toward the end of the match, the fans booed a frustrated Zbyszko. Unable to throw Hackenschmidt, Zbyszko butted with his head and struck Hackenschmidt with his elbows. After ninety minutes, the referee declared Zbyszko the winner since Hackenschmidt failed to throw Zbyszko once much less twice.^{ccxx}

Zbyszko's victory should have guaranteed him a rematch with Gotch. In what became an infuriating situation, Gotch ignored Zbyszko's win and signed to wrestle Hackenschmidt on Labor Day 1911 in Chicago, Illinois. Would Gotch ever wrestle Zbyszko again?

Figure 25-Stanislaus Zbyszko in 1910

Chapter 8 – Continuing to Pursue Gotch

Zbyszko continued to pursue a rematch despite the frustration of Gotch's constant refusal to wrestle him again. Gotch and Zbyszko were on different paths in their professional wrestling careers.

Stanislaus Zbyszko, born on April 1, 1880, was only three years younger than Gotch. Zbyszko wrestled until 1925, when he was forty-five years old. He also won two world titles in the worked era.

Ed "Strangler" Lewis considered him one of only two wrestlers, who could beat Lewis, even though Zbyszko was over forty years old. Promoters forced Zbyszko to retire after one of the most famous double-crosses in professional wrestling history.[ccxxi]

Frank Gotch, born on April 27, 1877, was contemplating retirement to please his wife and because years of touring had taken a toll on his body. Gotch found an interim solution from 1911 to 1913. Gotch retired on active duty.

After he wrestled Zbyszko in June 1910, Gotch wrestled a handful of competitive matches with opponents he knew he could beat. He worked his matches in 1911 and 1912 with a handful of exceptions. Risking defeat to an able opponent like Zbyszko was not part of Gotch's late career plans.

Zbyszko had not given up on a rematch with Gotch yet. His Polish compatriots supported Zbyszko in his desire to secure a match with Gotch. A group of Chicago businesspeople of Polish descent put up $20,000 as an inducement for Gotch to get back into the ring with Zbyszko.[ccxxii] Gotch's camp expressed interest but not until Gotch dispatched Hackenschmidt.

While trying to tempt Gotch, Zbyszko gave an old foe a chance at redemption. After his embarrassing loss in January, John Lemm wanted a rematch with Zbyszko. Newspaper across the country carried accounts of the match leaving Lemm looking foolish for falling with Zbyszko on top of him in a pinning position. Zbyszko granted him a rematch in Chicago, Illinois on March 6, 1911.[ccxxiii]

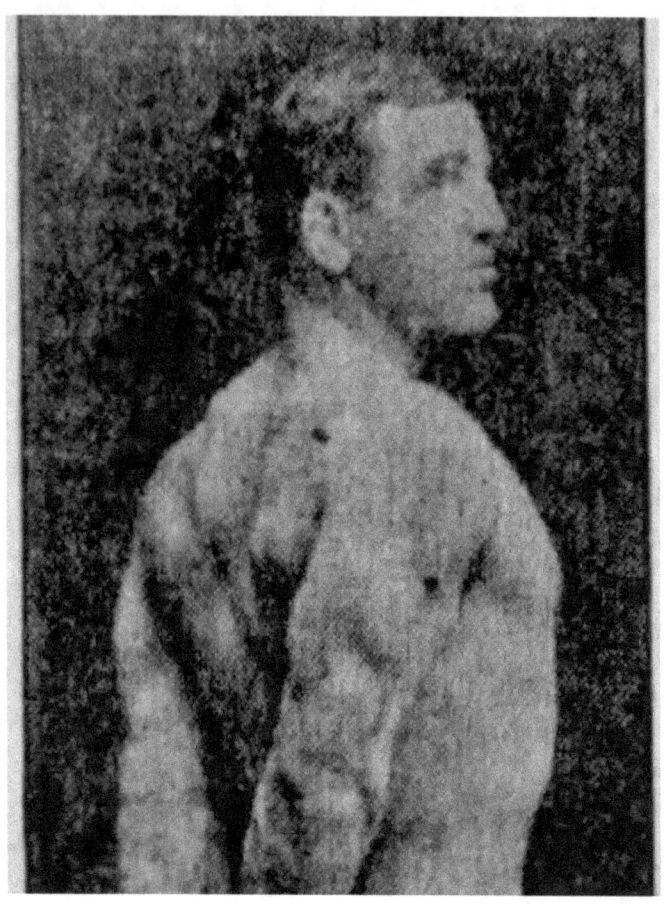

Figure 26- John Lemm's photo from the Detroit Times in 1911 (Public Domain)

Lemm at least redeemed himself in this match. Lemm pushed the pace for the first hour remaining on the offensive. Zbyszko was content to power out of Lemm's holds and look for an opening.

After fifty-four minutes, Zbyszko saw an opportunity and pounced. Grabbing Lemm in a reverse body hold, Zbyszko flipped Lemm to the mat for the first fall at 54 minutes, 10 seconds.[ccxxiv]

Lemm still appeared fresh after the ten-minute intermission. He pressed Zbyszko for over twenty minutes until Zbyszko took him to the mat. Zbyszko demonstrated his improving catch wrestling ability by using a head scissors to take the second fall in 27 minutes.[ccxxv]

On March 15, 1911, the problem with legitimate contests reared its head in a match between Stanislaus Zbyszko and Dr. Benjamin Roller. They wrestled each other in a deadly dull bout at Grand Rapids, Michigan.[ccxxvi]

Being equal in skill, the men stalemated each other for prolonged periods. Zbyszko won the first fall in 1 hour, 16 minutes.[ccxxvii]

Zbyszko needed only 12 minutes to pin the exhausted Roller for the second fall.[ccxxviii] Zbyszko did win the match in two straight falls, but fans and reporters booed the boring match.

On March 18th, Zbyszko wrestled Henry Ordeman in nearby Detroit.[ccxxix] Gotch's one-time protégé frequently wrestled Zbyszko during the latter's tour between 1910 and 1914. While Ordeman outlasted Zbyszko in handicapped matches, Zbyszko normally won the straight wrestling matches.

Ordeman favored the body hold but struggled to apply it to

Zbyszko's short, stout frame. Zbyszko weighed about 245 pounds for this bout.^{ccxxx}

Zbyszko used the scissors hold, a catch hold Zbyszko favored in his recent matches, to score the first fall on Ordeman. It took Zbyszko 1 hour, 35 minutes to pin Ordeman.^{ccxxxi}

The crowd protested the decision. Due to the men's position on the mat, sizable portions of the crowd could not see the fall.^{ccxxxii}

Figure 27-Henry Ordeman from 1910 (Public Domain)

However, the reporter for the *Detroit Free Press* agreed with Referee Karl that Zbyszko scored a fall. Ordeman accepted the decision which ended the controversy.[ccxxxiii]

At the start of the second fall, Zbyszko put Ordeman in a half-Nelson and crotch hold combination.

He worked Ordeman's shoulders to the mat pinning Ordeman at the 12-minute mark. Zbyszko beat two capable opponents in three days' time.^{ccxxxiv}

At the end of March, Stanislaus Zbyszko made news of a different sort. He expressed his desire to join the Polish diplomatic corps after he retired from professional wrestling. Zbyszko claimed to have made $150,000 in his wrestling career and was well off in retirement.^{ccxxxv} If Zbyszko made $150,000 in his career, he did not have Gotch and the pitiful title match payout to thank for it.

Zbyszko wrestled and defeated Dr. Roller again in Wichita, Kansas. He also defeated Joe "Yankee" Rogers in New York. After wrestling one more match in New York City resulting in an easy two fall victory of Andre Kandrat, Zbyszko sailed home for Poland on May 23, 1911. Zbyszko did not return to the United States until October 1911.^{ccxxxvi}

By the time he returned, Gotch had wrestled Hackenschmidt on Labor Day in Chicago. After collecting his last big pay day, Gotch was ready to ride off into the sunset. Zbyszko was not ready to give up yet. Could he lure Gotch with a big enough pay day?

Figure 28- Stanislaus Zbyszko in 1911 (Public Domain)

Chapter 9 – Zbyszko Returns from His Summer Vacation

Before Stanislaus Zbyszko returned from his vacation in Poland, his manager Jack Herman offered $10,000 as Zbyszko's part of a purse for a rematch with Frank Gotch. Herman also put up $1,000 as a forfeit, if Zbyszko failed to live up to the terms of the agreement.[ccxxxvii]

Gotch revealed his hesitancy to wrestle Zbyszko again in a meeting with Jack Herman in Humboldt, Iowa. Herman traveled to Gotch's hometown hoping to gain a commitment from Gotch to defend his title against Zbyszko.[ccxxxviii]

Herman offered to leave $1,000 with Gotch, which he could keep if Zbyszko did not meet the terms of their agreement. Gotch told Herman that he would wrestle Zbyszko only if he defeated Henry Ordeman, Joe Rogers, Jess Westergaard, and "Americus" Gus Schoenlein.[ccxxxix]

Zbyszko already defeated all the listed wrestlers, so Herman did not hesitate to accept the list of contenders. He even offered to Gotch that he could keep the $1,000, if Zbyszko failed to beat any wrestler on Gotch's list of contenders.[ccxl]

Gotch refused to commit himself that much. He returned the $1,000 to Herman. He made a "half promise" to consider Zbyszko if he beat the men. Gotch did not refuse outright to wrestle Zbyszko again which encouraged Herman to continue pursuing the rematch.[ccxli]

Zbyszko arrived back in the United States on the steamer *Augusta Victoria*. The ship made port in New York City on October 28, 1911.

Zbyszko deposited his $10,000 portion of the purse for a Gotch rematch in New York City.[ccxlii]

For Zbyszko's first big match back, he signed to wrestle Italian strongman Giovanni Raicevich. In a move that continued to frustrate Zbyszko, Frank Gotch agreed to wrestle the winner of the match.[ccxliii] After Zbyszko won one of these matches, Gotch developed amnesia about the statement he or Klank made to the newspapers.

Figure 29-Raicevich with arms crossed (Public Domain)

Tom Jenkins, the former American Heavyweight Champion, refereed the bout scheduled for Christmas Day at Madison Square Garden. Raicevich's fans questioned Jenkins' actions after the contest.[ccxliv]

4,000 fans filed into Madison Square Gardens for the big match. The crowd consisted primarily of New Yorkers of Italian and Polish descent.[ccxlv]

Zbyszko agreed to throw Raicevich three times within the 90-minute time limit. If Raicevich scored one fall, Jenkins would award him the match.[ccxlvi]

Zbyszko took the first fall with a cross arm hold at 37 minutes, 50 seconds. The men took a ten-minute rest before starting the second fall. The controversy arose in the second fall.[ccxlvii]

Raicevich threw Zbyszko to the match with a crotch hold. However, both men landed partially off the mat. Zbyszko relaxed expecting Jenkins to move them to the center of the ring. Raicevich took advantage of Zbyszko's position and turned him into a pin with a half-Nelson even though they were off the mat.[ccxlviii]

Jenkins tapped Raicevich on the back and told him that he was moving the men to the center of the mat. Raicevich mistook Jenkins' action as the signal that he pinned Zbyszko. He jumped to his feet in celebration.[ccxlix]

Jenkins tried to explain to Raicevich that he did not pin Zbyszko legally. Zbyszko also tried to keep Raicevich in the ring by dragging on his arm. Raicevich did not pay attention to either of them.[ccl]

Raicevich jumped into the arms of his supporters who carried him around the arena on their shoulders. It took five minutes for Jenkins to explain what happened to

Raicevich's manager and get Raicevich back to the ring.[ccli]

When Jenkins explained the situation to Raicevich, Raicevich refused to return to the ring and left with his cornermen.[cclii] Jenkins awarded the match to Zbyszko by forfeit as Raicevich refused to return.

New York Police escorted Jenkins and Zbyszko to the back as the crowd reacted violently to the decision. The crowd did not riot but it took the police thirty minutes to clear the arena. Fans threw seat cushions and broke furniture as they left but they did not injure anyone.[ccliii]

After throwing his tantrum, Raicevich reconsidered his actions. He asked Zbyszko for a rematch. Herman agreed if Raicevich put up $5,000 for his half of the $10,000, winner take all purse. Raicevich deposited his half with a New York newspaper office.[ccliv]

Out of desperation over his failure to secure a rematch, Zbyszko started claiming the World Title based on Gotch's stated desire to retire. Zbyszko offered $10,000 for his half of a title match purse.[cclv] Neither fans nor reporters recognized his claims and no wrestlers stepped forward for the "title match."

Figure 30- Jesse Westergaard misidentified as Stanislaus Zbyszko in the January 10, 1912, Salt Lake Tribune (Public Domain)

Zbyszko's first big match of 1912 would be a rematch with Jess Westergaard. Westergaard outlasted Zbyszko in another handicap match on December 28, 1911, in Knoxville, Tennessee.[cclvi]

The men met in Salt Lake City, Utah. Zbyszko desperately wanted to beat Westergaard to establish himself as the next challenger for Gotch.[cclvii] Westergaard did not make it easy for Zbyszko.

Westergaard entered the ring at 212 pounds. Zbyszko weighed 236 pounds for the match. After Referee Julius Johnson started the match, Zbyszko wrestled defensively for the first thirty minutes. Westergaard used his long arms on Zbyszko's short legs to secure the toehold three times.[cclviii]

Zbyszko kicked out of the toehold each time to the boos of the crowd. Crowds did not normally boo Zbyszko, who resented the fans' negative reaction.[cclix]

Zbyszko charged Westergaard and took him down with a double leg takedown. He tried to turn

Westergaard for at least five minutes before Westergaard escaped back to his feet.[cclx]

Westergaard took Zbyszko back down and tried to turn him. To Westergaard's surprise, Zbyszko picked him up from a kneeling position and dumped Westergaard on his head. Westergaard tried to bridge but Zbyszko grabbed his far arm, pinned it to Westergaard's side and pressed his shoulders to the mat.[cclxi] Zbyszko gained the first fall after 1 hour, 2 minutes.

The men rested for ten minutes before Referee Johnson started the second fall. Zbyszko intended to make it a short one.

Zbyszko picked Westergaard up with a double-leg takedown, dumped Westergaard to the mat and put on a reverse body hold. Over the next five minutes, Zbyszko slowly turned

Westergaard to his back and lowered his shoulder to the mat for the second fall at 7 minutes, 11 seconds.[cclxii] Zbyszko beat the tough contender in two straight falls.

Westergaard told reporters, "He is too big for me."[cclxiii] Westergaard remained a tough challenge for Zbyszko though. He and Ordeman trouble Zbyszko more than other wrestlers.

Figure 31-Zbyszko Wrestling an Opponent in 1911 (Public Domain)

On January 16, 1912, Zbyszko faced another frequent foe, Henry Ordeman, in Ordeman's hometown of

Minneapolis, Minnesota. It was another two-out-of-three falls match.[cclxiv]

The men wrestled at the Minneapolis Auditorium. Frank Force refereed the contest. The men entered the ring, shook hands, and prepared to wrestle.

Henry Ordeman took the offensive to start the match by pushing Zbyszko around the ring.[cclxv] Ordeman's mentor Frank Gotch used a similar tactic against Zbyszko during their 1910 match.

At the ten-minute mark, Ordeman dove for Zbyszko's leg, lifted it up for a single leg takedown and dumped Zbyszko to the mat. Zbyszko scrambled back to his feet.[cclxvi]

Ordeman managed to get Zbyszko back to the mat, where he applied a leg scissors to Zbyszko's head as he attempted to apply a toehold at the same time. In a move reminiscent of his match with Westergaard, Zbyszko lifted Ordeman off the mat, while Zbyszko was still kneeling, and rolled over with Ordeman. Zbyszko used the scissors and reverse Nelson to pin Ordeman at 25 minutes, 25 seconds.^{cclxvii}

The men rested during the ten-minute intermission. Ordeman pushed the action trying to tie the bout up at one fall apiece.

He took Zbyszko down at the 25-minute mark. Ordeman secured a toehold, but he could not submit Zbyszko. Zbyszko pulled his foot away from Ordeman by brute strength alone.^{cclxviii}

At the 35-minutes mark, Ordeman secured another toehold. Zbyszko again powered out and rolled over on top of Ordeman. Zbyszko worked for five minutes before he was able to lock on a body hold and half-Nelson. Zbyszko forced Ordeman's shoulders to the mat at 48 minutes, 15 seconds.^{cclxix}

Zbyszko won the match in two straight falls, but he did not escape the match unscathed. Zbyszko iced his sore and swollen right ankle, the victim of Ordeman's toeholds.^{cclxx}

After negotiating for three weeks, the camps of Stanislaus Zbyszko and Giovanni Raicevich agreed to a rematch at Madison Square Garden on February 12, 1912. The wrestlers divided the $10,000 with the winner receiving eighty percent. Raicevich also gave Zbyszko $1,000 for agreeing to the rematch.^{cclxxi}

Raicevich made one demand. The referee must speak Italian. Famed opera singer Enrico Caruso told the newspapers he could help find a suitable referee for his compatriot.^{cclxxii}

In the end, Tom Jenkins refereed the rematch, but an interpreter conveyed Jenkins' instructions to Raicevich. The men shook hands as Jenkins started the match at 10:19 p.m.^{cclxxiii}

Raicevich did well at the start of the bout. After each man bulled the other around the ring, Raicevich slipped behind Zbyszko. He lifted Zbyszko up and dumped him to the mat, but Zbyszko immediately rolled up to his feet.^{cclxxiv}

Raicevich followed Zbyszko, grabbed his head and threw him over his shoulder with a flying mare. Zbyszko rolled up to his feet again.^{cclxxv}

Raicevich slipped behind Zbyszko again and tried two rolling falls, but Zbyszko dropped his center of gravity preventing the throw. Zbyszko broke Raicevich's grip. Zbyszko fouled Raicevich by head butting his nose, but Raicevich did not retaliate.[cclxxvi]

Zbyszko slipped to Raicevich's back, but Raicevich grabbed an armbar forcing Zbyszko to release his grip. Raicevich kept the armbar. Zbyszko realized his arm was in danger and flung Raicevich sideways while pulling with his arm. The quick move thwarted Raicevich's submission.[cclxxvii]

Zbyszko lifted Raicevich with a crotch hold and slammed him to the mat. Raicevich bridged out of danger and stood back on his feet.[cclxxviii] After thirty minutes of wrestling, Raicevich began to fatigue.

Zbyszko noticed his opponent's change in demeanor and attacked with two toeholds. Raicevich pulled out of both holds but with difficulty.[cclxxix]

At the fifty-minute mark, Zbyszko secured an odd but effective combination. Zbyszko secured a half-Nelson, crotch hold and leg lock combination. Zbyszko's leg lock put noticeable pressure on Raicevich's knee.[cclxxx]

As Raicevich grimaced as he was unable to free his leg, Zbyszko slowly lowered Raicevich's shoulders for the first fall at 54 minutes, 52 seconds.[cclxxxi] Zbyszko jumped to his feet, but Raicevich remained sitting on the mat.

Raicevich slowly got to his feet but limped to his corner. His cornermen helped Raicevich to the back. He could not walk back by himself.^{cclxxxii}

After ten minutes, Raicevich failed to return to the ring. His seconds informed referee Tom Jenkins that Raicevich could not continue. They believed Raicevich suffered a dislocated knee but could not say for certain until a doctor examined him.^{cclxxxiii}

For the first time since coming to America in 1909, Zbyszko injured an opponent with a submission hold. Zbyszko did not start training seriously in catch wrestling until 1910. Zbyszko's focus on learning a fresh style paid off in the addition of submission holds to his repertoire.

Zbyszko defeated other wrestlers over the next two months, but he was not any closer to securing a match with Frank Gotch.

Zbyszko was so desperate to secure a rematch that he agreed to wrestle Yussif Mahmout. He refused to wrestle Mahmout in 1911 based on their checkered history in Europe.

After Gotch tentatively agreed to wrestle the winner of the match, Jack Herman agreed to a match in Chicago between Zbyszko and Mahmout.[cclxxxiv] Gotch's manager Emil Klank also managed Mahmout. However, Gotch rescinded the agreement to face the winner, so the match fell through.

Jack Herman received a tentative agreement for Frank Gotch to wrestle Stanislaus Zbyszko at the Elks Convention in Portland, Oregon between July 8-13, 1912.[cclxxxv] Zbyszko posted $1,000 forfeit for Gotch. He also agreed to stay in the United States for the summer. Gotch refused to sign the agreement.[cclxxxvi]

Tired of Gotch backing out of each agreement, Zbyszko went home to Poland for the summer. By now, he must know that Gotch would not give him a rematch. Would he come back to the United States for another campaign in 1912-1913?

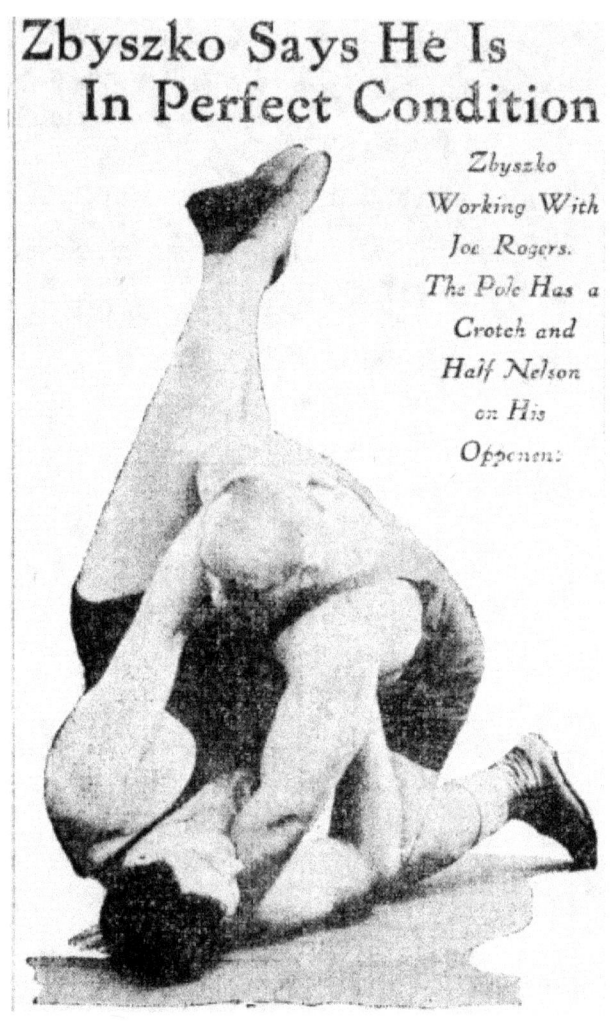

Figure 32- Stanislaus Zbyszko Wrestling Joe "Yankee" Rogers in 1912 (Public Domain)

Chapter 10 – Frank Gotch Retires

Newspaper kept referring to Frank Gotch as retired in 1912. However, Gotch wrestled nine matches in 1912. He wrestled seven matches in March 1912 alone. However, he was retired after a fashion.

Gotch wrestled protégé Henry Ordeman three times, former training partners Marin Plestina twice and Jess Westergaard once.[cclxxxvii] In fact, I believe Gotch wrestled one legitimate contest and I am not sure about after he defeated Georg Hackenschmidt in 1911.

I suspected Gotch and "Americus" Gus Schoenlein worked their match on June 14, 1912, in Baltimore, Maryland.[cclxxxviii] Gotch and "Americus" worked matches with each other in the past. However, "Americus" helped Georg Hackenschmidt train for his 1911 match with Gotch.

Gotch wrestled "Americus" in Oriole Ball Park for the June 1912 match. Promoters expected a large crowd to turn out to see hometown hero "Americus" wrestle Gotch.[cclxxxix]

After about an hour of wrestling, Gotch took "Americus" down. Gotch aggressively applied the toehold forcing "Americus" to submit at 62 minutes, 10 seconds.[ccxc]

After the ten-minute intermission, "Americus" returned to the ring barefoot with a visibly swollen ankle. He tried to wrestle the second fall, but Gotch grabbed the toehold at the signal to start. "Americus" tapped immediately before Gotch could apply any pressure.[ccxci]

Gotch had not wrestled a professional match for three months before the "Americus" match. In preparing for contests, Gotch often trained for two to three months. Because he took time off prior to the match and the toehold caused visible swelling on Schoenlein's ankle, Gotch may not have been "working" with "Americus."

Gotch did wrestle one more contest in his last match as World Heavyweight Wrestling Champion. Gotch picked a foreign wrestler from Eastern Europe for his final match. Stanislaus Zbyszko was not the wrestler.

The Estonia region of the Russian Empire produced one great wrestler, one exceptionally good wrestler and one good wrestler between 1897 and 1899. George Hackenschmidt was the great wrestler. Aleksander "Alex" Aberg was the exceptionally good wrestler.

Gotch chose to wrestle the good wrestler, Georg Lurich, in his final match. Born on April 10, 1876, the 36-year-old Lurich was a year older than Gotch. Standing five feet, ten inches tall and weighing two hundred pounds, Lurich was about the same size as Gotch.[ccxcii]

For his final match, Gotch wrestled Lurich at the Convention Hall in Kansas City. Outside of Chicago, Gotch often drew the biggest crowds in Kansas City. 12,000 fans filled the Convention Hall to see Gotch's retirement match.[ccxciii]

Figure 33- George Lurich around 1905 (Public Domain)

Prior to the start of the match, the ring announcer introduced Stanislaus Zbyszko to the crowd. The announcer stated Zbyszko would wrestle the winner of this match.[ccxciv] Or so everyone thought.

After the customary handshake, the men tied up to start the match at 10:27 p.m. Within two minutes, Gotch took Lurich's back and worked for a toehold. Unable to secure the toehold, he switched to a half-Nelson.[ccxcv]

Lurich broke the half-Nelson, but Gotch immediately reapplied it. Lurich broke and Gotch applied three half-Nelsons before he switched to a different tactic.[ccxcvi]

Gotch secured his pet move, the toehold. Lurich bucked like a donkey to free his foot.[ccxcvii] Lurich feared the damage Gotch's grip could do.

Gotch let Lurich think he was going for a crotch hold and half-Nelson, one of Gotch's favorite combinations. Lurich started to turn to escape, when Gotch flowed into a hammerlock. Gotch released the hammerlock enough to let Lurich attempt an escape. Gotch then secured an armlock and toehold combination, a rare combo that only Gotch employed.[ccxcviii]

Gotch used this combo to pin Lurich for the first fall. Gotch needed only 18 minutes, 10 seconds for the first fall.[ccxcix]

Gotch toyed with Lurich in a painful way during the second fall. Gotch slammed Lurich to the mat so hard twice that Lurich bounced off the mat. Dazed from the impact of two hard slams, Gotch easily applied a full-Nelson to Lurich. Gotch pinned Lurich for the second fall at 5 minutes, 35 seconds.[ccc] The soon-to-be 35-year-old Gotch retired after the match.

Fans know professional wrestlers often retire to unretire within a year or two. Gotch stayed retired. Other than a brief flirtation with working a match with Joe Stecher, Gotch made appearances on vaudeville and raised hogs in Humboldt. Gotch did not wrestle anymore legitimate contests.

Promoters and wrestlers continued challenging Gotch after his retirement. Tired of the constant challenges, Gotch agreed to anoint Joe Stecher as his successor by losing a worked match in the fall of 1915.

A worked match between Gotch and Bobby Managoff, Sr. in preparation for the Stecher match ended these plans. Even though they were working, Gotch broke his leg after his foot caught in a loose mat. Fans accepted Stecher even without a victory over Gotch ending the constant challenges to Gotch.

Frank Gotch finally had peace. Stanislaus Zbyszko never secured the rematch with Frank Gotch.

Figure 34-Gotch Securing His Arm Hold and Toehold in 1913 (Public Domain)

Chapter 11 – Zbyszko Returns to Europe in 1914

Stanislaus Zbyszko returned to the United States at the end of 1912 thinking Gotch would finally wrestle him again after dispatching Lurich. It was not to be.

Stanislaus Zbyszko welcomed his younger brother, Wladek, to the United States in March 1913. Born in 1891, the 22-year-old Wladek was eleven years younger than Stanislaus.

Unlike Stanislaus, who returned to Poland each summer, Wladek remained in the United States. Only traveling back to Poland once in 1922 to see his sick mother, Wladek Zbyszko rarely left the United States unless he was touring South America in the 1930s.

Wladek Zbyszko died in the United Sates in 1968.

Stanislaus Zbyszko continued to travel back and forth to Poland but before he left in 1913, he wrestled a couple of controversial matches in May 1913.

During a match with Constant Lemarin in Montreal, Quebec, Canada on May 24, 1913, Zbyszko and Lemarin fell from the ring. Zbyszko suffered a cut above his eye and a concussion.

The referee disqualified Lemarin for pushing Zbyszko from the ring. The ringside doctor refused to let Zbyszko continue so the referee awarded the match to Zbyszko for the foul.[ccci]

The doctor told Zbyszko to take four weeks off training and wrestling. Zbyszko thanked him and ignored the advice. Herman booked

Zbyszko in a match with Georg Lurich, Gotch's last title opponent, at Madison Square Garden in New York City. Zbyszko refused to no-show the bout.

Zbyszko entered the ring with a large bandage wrapped around his head. Knowing his compromised condition, Zbyszko attacked from the opening bell of the May 28th bout.

Zbyszko threw Lurich to the mat with a flying mare. Zbyszko secured a half-Nelson and reverse body hold. Zbyszko worked to turn Lurich over.[cccii]

Zbyszko suddenly fell on his side as his body went limp. Lurich did not realize Zbyszko fainted and started to turn Zbyszko onto his back. However, referee Charlie White saw Zbyszko faint. He pulled Lurich off Zbyszko, awarded Lurich the first fall and directed Zbyszko's corner men to help him to the corner.^{ccciii}

After he regained consciousness, Stanislaus' corner men and Wladek Zbyszko, who wrestled earlier on the card, helped Stanislaus Zbyszko to the dressing room. The doctor refused to let Stanislaus Zbyszko continue. White awarded the match to Lurich.^{ccciv}

Lurich said he refused to accept the victory under such conditions. He offered Stanislaus Zbyszko a rematch once he recovered.^{cccv}

When he returned to the United States in 1921, Stanislaus Zbyszko's promoters claimed Frank Gotch was the only wrestler to defeat Stanislaus Zbyszko in a singles match during his first tour of the United States. Zbyszko lost handicap matches. However, they claimed no one defeated him in singles matches other than Gotch.

While we cannot give Georg Lurich full marks for his victory, Lurich holds a win over Zbyszko in a singles match. Zbyszko lost two singles matches during his first tour of American between 1909 and 1914.

In 1914, Zbyszko finally accepted Gotch would never give him a rematch. Before he returned to Poland, Stanislaus Zbyszko wrestled a match that shaped the American wrestling landscape even after Zbyszko returned to Europe.

Stanislaus Zbyszko wrestled Aleksander "Alex" Aberg for the World Heavyweight Greco-Roman Wrestling Championship. Aberg claimed the title based on European tournament victories from the previous year. Promoter George Touhey billed Aberg as Finnish although the following year Aberg and Lurich represented Russia in the 1915 New York International Wrestling Tournament.[cccvi]

5,000 fans filled the Mechanic's Building in Boston to see the match.[cccvii] The match drew a good crowd for a style of wrestling not popular in the U.S.

In Greco-Roman wrestling, the rules ban holds below the waist. For the first hour, the evenly matched opponents remained in a tie-up aggravating the crowd with the lack of action.[cccviii]

After an hour, Zbyszko took Aberg to the mat and applied a back hold. Aberg pulled out of the hold but was on his hip. Zbyszko used a cross-body hold to pin Aberg for the first fall at 1 hour, 2 minutes and 45 seconds.[cccix]

Down one fall, Aberg attacked from the start of the second. Both Aberg and Zbyszko slipped out of multiple hold attempts before Aberg picked Zbyszko off the mat with a waist hold, slammed him to the mat and turned Zbyszko onto his back with a half-Nelson. The referee awarded Aberg the second fall at 35 minutes, 25 seconds.[cccx]

Zbyszko looked surprised but prepared for the third and deciding fall. Fans in Boston saw only the second man to pin Zbyszko during his five-year tour of America.

Zbyszko did not give Aberg a chance in the third fall. Zbyszko threw Aberg to the mat three times with flying mares. After throwing Aberg the last time, Zbyszko used a front bear hug to force Aberg's shoulders to the mat for the third fall in 35 seconds.^{cccxi}

Aberg furiously jumped to his feet. He tackled Zbyszko from behind and tried to force his shoulders to the mat. As Zbyszko looked on incredulously, the referee attempted to pull Aberg off, but Aberg was too strong. A Boston Police Officer entered the ring, told Aberg to release Zbyszko and go back to his corner. Aberg let go and obeyed the officer's commands.^{cccxii}

Figure 35- Artist Rendering of the Match from the February 27, 1914, Boston Globe (Public Domain)

When I wrote about this match on my blog around 2015, a reader left a comment stating that promoters paid Aberg $10,000 to drop the match to Zbyszko. I found this story unbelievable and asked for a source for this information. To date, I have not received this information. The economics involved convince me the story is not true.

When the 1915 New York International Wrestling Tournament occurred the following year, promoter Sam Rachmann charged between fifty cents and two dollars for tickets. If we use the high-ticket price of $2.00 for 5,000 fans, Touhey paid his entire gate of $10,000 to Aberg to lose the match.

Gambling is the other significant source of income during this era. A specialty wrestling match with an unknown wrestler does not draw big bets. From a business and financial perspective, Touhey paying Aberg to lose, particularly such a large amount, is ridiculous on the face of it.

Second, Aberg traveled to the United States to challenge Frank Gotch. When Gotch refused his challenge, his promoter Sam Rachmann staged the 1915 New York tournament to replace Gotch with Aberg as champion. Aberg would not knowingly lose a bout when his goal was for the fans to recognize him as World Champion.

Finally, in 1917, Aberg sued New York promoter Jack Curley. Under oath, Aberg admitted to working matches in 1916 for Curley's cards until he realized American fans hated "faking". Aberg testified that he wrestled only in legitimate contests other than this handful of matches.[cccxiii] Aberg swore he wrestled contests with Stanislaus Zbyszko and his opponents in the 1915 New York International wrestling tournament.

Stanislaus Zbyszko defeated Aberg in a contest. He was now the recognized Greco-Roman Wrestling World Champion.

Zbyszko wrestled one more match with Henry Ordeman before returning to Poland. Ordeman shocked Zbyszko and the fans in the first fall of their May 15th match in Minneapolis.

Zbyszko preferred to wrestle barefoot. Ordeman wrung a concession from Zbyszko to wear wrestling shoes for the match or forfeit $500.00. Zbyszko agreed.[cccxiv]

Ordeman, Gotch's protégé, wanted Zbyszko to wear shoes because it would be easier for Ordeman to apply the toehold. Ordeman secured a toehold and forced Zbyszko to submit at the 26-minute mark.[cccxv] Three opponents pinned or submitted

Zbyszko only four times during the previous five years.

In disgust, Zbyszko ripped his wrestling shoes off and threw them from the ring. He told Ordeman he could have the $500.00.[cccxvi]

Zbyszko wrestled like a man possessed in the next two falls. He won the second fall with a head scissors and crotch hold in 13 minutes, 14 seconds. Zbyszko finished Ordeman off for the third fall by pinning him with a half-Nelson and crotch hold combination in 33 minutes.[cccxvii]

After this match, Zbyszko returned to Europe. He did not return to the United States until 1921, when he was 41 years old. Zbyszko's impact on American wrestling was not over though.

When Zbyszko returned to Poland, World War I raged in Europe.

By November 1914, Stanislaus Zbyszko enlisted as a 2ⁿᵈ Lieutenant in the Austrian Army.[cccxviii] Zbyszko fought in major battles and spent time as a prisoner of war.

After the Armistice, Zbyszko traveled back to Poland. He tried to secure a passport to return to the United States. It took him two years and the assistance of a U.S. Senator to make it back.

Promoter Sam Rachmann conveniently forgot Stanislaus Zbyszko defeated Aberg for the World Heavyweight Greco-Roman Wrestling Championship. Rachmann claimed that Stanislaus gave his title to Wladek before he returned to Poland.

When fans rejected this explanation, Rachmann claimed Stanislaus Zbyszko vacated the championship when he returned to Poland. Rachmann never mentioned

Zbyszko defeating Aberg the previous year.

Stanislaus Zbyszko never shared his thoughts about the 1915 New York International Wrestling Tournament as he was fighting a war. Wladek Zbyszko emerged as the leading contender to challenge Aberg in the tournament.[cccxix]

Figure 36-Zbyszko Catch Wrestling (Public Domain)

Conclusion

If you only read this book, this period of his career a distorted view of Frank Gotch as a World Champion and competitor. Gotch was the best wrestler in the world between 1905 and 1910. He defeated Georg Hackenschmidt, Tom Jenkins, and Stanislaus Zbyszko, when all three men were in their prime.

When he defeated Zbyszko, Gotch was 33 years old. Being the best in the world exerts tremendous pressure on an athlete. Everyone trains to beat the champion. Gotch always had to be at his best.

Combat Sports World Champions reign for one to two years on average. Knowing he was getting older, and particularly after marrying Gladys in 1911, Gotch decided to wind down his career. This decision affected Stanislaus Zbyszko the most.

We will never know if Stanislaus Zbyszko could defeat Frank Gotch in a rematch. We do know that Gotch ducked Zbyszko's challenge for three years even though it would be Gotch's biggest payday.

Gotch consistently refused to wrestle Zbyszko while feigning interest to protect his reputation. In the book *Frank A. Gotch: World Champion's Wrestler* by George Sanders Robbins, which Gotch assisted in writing and approved, Robbins pokes fun at Zbyszko's challenge.

"For a year or two past Zbyszko has been making considerable noise in the hope of securing another match with Gotch and the accompanying large consignment of American dollars via a share in the gate receipts. His aspirations in this direction have not achieved serious consideration."[cccxx]

Robbins further included quotes from friendly journalists dismissing Zbyszko's claims. In general, the American press consistently provided Gotch positive coverage but there were exceptions.

On March 6, 1912, the *Evening Times* of Grand Forks, North Dakota stated the obvious in a headline "Gotch Afraid to Wrestle Pole".[cccxxi] It was unusual for the Midwestern press to hold Gotch's feet to the fire. However, Gotch's ducking of Zbyszko was so blatant, the friendly press could no longer ignore it.

Frank Gotch should have wrestled Zbyszko again no later than the summer of 1912. For reasons we will never know, he refused to do so. Gotch only ducked one wrestler, Stanislaus Zbyszko, in his career. While Gotch still stands as the greatest legitimate wrestler in American history, we cannot ignore this chapter of his career. Stanislaus Zbyszko deserved better.

Figure 37-Stanislaus Zbyszko in 1913 (Public Domain)

Epilogue

Frank Alvin Gotch did not enjoy a long retirement. Gotch planned to raise prize hogs on his Humboldt, Iowa farm and tour vaudeville after retiring from the ring.

One year into his retirement, Gladys gave birth to Frank Robert Gotch. Frank Robert was Frank's and Gladys' only son. Everyone said Frank and Gladys doted on Frank Robert.

Four years into retirement, the 40-year-old Gotch sought treatment at a Chicago hospital.[cccxxii] Doctors diagnosed kidney trouble and initially thought he would recover quickly.

Gotch and his wife Gladys were supposed to leave for Hot Springs, Arkansas to recover but Gotch was still in the hospital at the end of

October 1917. Doctors said he was improving greatly and should leave within the next week.[cccxxiii]

Gotch remained in the hospital and newspapers carried stories saying Gotch may be in grave condition. On November 9, 1917, a *Chicago Eagle* reporter called the hospital to check on Gotch's condition.

The reporter asked the man who answered the phone, "Is Gotch's condition serious?" The man replied, "Rats, no. And, furthermore, if they don't let me out of her soon, I'm going to pull a Douglas Fairbanks and escape."[cccxxiv]

When the reporter asked who he was talking to, the man replied, "Gotch himself. Frank Gotch; I'm not sick at all."[cccxxv]

The reporter said he heard Gotch was dying of kidney disease. Gotch said, "Zatso? Well, I have a kink in my back from loading hogs back in Iowa."[cccxxvi] It must have been difficult for someone, who had been in elite condition most of his adult life, to accept he was seriously ill.

On December 16, 1917, Frank Gotch died at his home in Humboldt, Iowa from uremic poisoning. Gotch suffered from kidney trouble for two years but hid it from the public.[cccxxvii] In October 1917, the progression of the illness forced him to seek medical treatment. It eventually took his life. The family interred Gotch in the family mausoleum at Union Cemetery in Humboldt, Iowa.

Stanislaus Zbyszko made a comeback in American during 1921.

Zbyszko wrestled until 1925 when the famous double-cross forced his retirement. Zbyszko came back for one match with the Great Gama in 1930, when Zbyszko was 50 years old.

Nearing sixty, Zbyszko wrestled matches in St. Louis during 1937 but his final comeback was short-lived. Zbyszko should have followed Gotch's example and stayed retired after 1925.

Zbyszko disappeared from the public eye until 1950, when he wrestled one of the most famous movie wrestling matches in the movie *Night and the City* (1950). The seventy-year-old wrestled Mike Mazurki in the film. Film historians consider it the best wrestling match in a movie.

Stanislaus Zbyszko spent the last years of his life living on his brother Wladek's farm in Savannah,

Missouri. 87-year-old Stanislaus Zbyszko died in the St. Joseph Hospital on September 22, 1967, from congestive heart failure. He had been sick for five days.

Wladek interred Stanislaus Zbyszko, a widower, in the Laurel Hills Cemetery in Saco, Maine. Stanislaus interred his deceased wife in the same cemetery before moving to the farm with Wladek and Wladek's wife. Zbyszko survived Gotch by 50 years.

Figure 38- This Photo Ran in Newspapers Across the Country in November 1917 Denying the Seriousness of Frank Gotch's Illness (Public Domain)

Other Combat Sports Books by Ken Zimmerman Jr.

Double-Crossing the Gold Dust Trio: Stanislaus Zbyszko's Last Hurrah

Masked Marvel To The Rescue: The Gimmick That Saved the 1915 New York Wrestling Tournament

Gotch vs. Hackenschmidt: The Matches That Made and Destroyed Legitimate American Professional Wrestling

Evan "The Strangler" Lewis: The Most Feared Wrestler of the 19th Century

William Muldoon: The Solid Man Conquers Wrestling and Physical Culture

Morrissey vs. Poole: Politics, Prizefighting and the Murder of Bill the Butcher

Bibliography

Newspapers

Alaska Daily Empire (Juneau, Alaska)

Arizona Republican (Phoenix, Arizona)

The Bemidji Daily Pioneer (Bemidji, Minnesota)

The Boston Globe (Boston, Massachusetts)

Bridgeport Times and Evening Farmer (Bridgeport, Connecticut)

Brooklyn Daily Eagle (Brooklyn, New York)

Buffalo Courier (Buffalo, New York)

Buffalo Enquirer (Buffalo, New York)

The Calumet News (Calumet, Michigan)

Chicago Eagle (Chicago, Illinois)

Chicago Tribune (Chicago, Illinois)

Commercial Appeal (Memphis, Tennessee)

The Daily Times (Davenport, Iowa)

Des Moines Register (Des Moines, Iowa)

Detroit Free Press (Detroit, Michigan)

The Detroit Times (Detroit, Michigan)

Evansville Press (Evansville, Indiana)

Evening Journal (Wilmington, Delaware)

The Evening News (Wilkes-Barre, Pennsylvania)

Evening Star (Washington, D.C.)

The Evening Times (Grand Forks, North Dakota)

The Fairmont West Virginian (Fairmont, West Virginia)

Fargo Forum and Daily Republican (Fargo, North Dakota)

Fulton County News (McConnelsburg,

Pennsylvania)

Herald and Review (Decatuer, Illinois)

The Kansas City Times (Kansas City, Missouri)

La Crosse Tribune (La Crosse, Wisconsin)

The Lake County Times (Hammond, Indiana)

Leavenworth Times (Leavenworth, Kansas)

Lincoln Journal Star (Lincoln, Nebraska)

Muscatine News Tribune (Muscatine, Iowa)

New York Times (New York, New York)

New York Tribune (New York, New York)

Norwich Bulletin (Norwich, Connecticut)

Ogden Standard (Ogden, Utah)

Oklahoma City Daily Pointer (Oklahoma City, Oklahoma)

Omaha Daily Bee (Omaha, Nebraska)

Ottawa Daily Republic (Ottawa, Kansas)

Ottumwa Tri-Weekly Courier (Ottumwa, Iowa)

Quad-City Times (Davenport, Iowa)

Philadelphia Inquirer (Philadelphia, Pennsylvania)

Pittston Gazette (Pittston, Pennsylvania)

Republican and Herald (Pottsville, Pennsylvania)

Rock Island Argus (Rock Island, Illinois)

Salina Daily Union (Salina, Kansas)

Salt Lake Tribune (Salt Lake City, Utah)

San Francisco Call (San Francisco, California)

Santa Cruz Sentinel (Santa Cruz, California)

Sedalia Democrat (Sedalia, Missouri)

Sioux City Journal (Sioux City, Iowa)

Star-Gazette (Elmira, New York)

Star Tribune (Minneapolis, Minnesota)

St. Louis Post-Dispatch (St. Louis, Missouri)

The Times (Munster, Indiana)

Times Union (Brooklyn, New York)

The Washington Herald (Washington, D.C.)

Washington Times (Washington, D.C.)

Wilkes-Barre Times Leader (Wilkes-Barre, Pennsylvania)

Books

Frank A. Gotch, World Champion's Wrestler: His Life, Mat Battles and Instructions on How to Wrestle by George Sanders Robbins

Gotch vs. Hackenschmidt: The Matches That Made and Destroyed

Legitimate American Professional Wrestling by Ken Zimmerman Jr.

Wrestling in the Garden, Volume 1: 1875-1939; The Battle for New York – Works, Shoots and Double-Crosses by Scott Teal and J. Michael Kenyon

Websites

www.wrestlingdata.com

www.newspapers.com

findagrave.com

legacyofwrestling.com

Missouri Death Certificate Database

About the Author

Ken Zimmerman Jr. is a married father and grandfather, who lives outside of St. Louis, Missouri. Ken has been interested in combat sports since watching professional wrestling from St. Louis in the late 1970s. His stepdad, Ernest Charles Diaz, who raised him, introduced him to boxing in 1981. A lifelong martial artist, Ken holds rank in three martial arts including a 4th Degree black belt in Taekwondo.

If you like this book, you can sign up for Ken's newsletter to receive information about future book releases. You can sign up for the newsletter and receive a bonus e-book by going to www.kenzimmermanjr.com and signing up for the newsletter.

Endnote

Introduction
[i] Frank A. Gotch, World's Champion Wrestler by George Sanders Robbins, p. 21

Chapter 1
[ii] Ottawa Daily Republic (Ottawa, Kansas), March 26, 1909, p. 1
[iii] Raoul de Rouen. Wrestlingdata.com
[iv] Ottawa Daily Republic (Ottawa, Kansas), March 26, 1909, p. 1
[v] Ibid
[vi] Omaha Daily Bee, March 28, 1909, p. 26
[vii] Ibid
[viii] Ibid
[ix] Ibid
[x] Chicago Tribune, April 15, 1909, p. 9
[xi] Ibid
[xii] Ibid
[xiii] Ibid
[xiv] Ibid
[xv] Ibid
[xvi] Ibid
[xvii] Ibid
[xviii] Ibid
[xix] Ibid
[xx] Ibid
[xxi] Ibid
[xxii] Ibid
[xxiii] Ibid
[xxiv] Ibid
[xxv] Ibid
[xxvi] Wrestlingdata.com
[xxvii] *Gotch vs. Hackenschmidt* (2016) by the author
[xxviii] Quad-City Times (Davenport, Iowa), April 21, 1909, p. 6
[xxix] The Daily Times (Davenport, Iowa), April 23, 1909, p. 8

[xxx] Sedalia Democrat (Sedalia, Missouri), April 28, 1909, p. 8
[xxxi] Ibid
[xxxii] The Commercial Appeal (Memphis, TN), April 30, 1909, p. 10
[xxxiii] Ibid
[xxxiv] Ibid
[xxxv] Salina Daily Union (Salina, KS), May 7, 1909, p. 1
[xxxvi] Ibid
[xxxvii] Frank A. Gotch by George Sanders Robbins, p. 22
[xxxviii] The Philadelphia Inquirer, May 28, 1909, p. 10
[xxxix] Frank A. Gotch by George Sanders Robbins
[xl] Star Tribune (Minneapolis, Minnesota), June 4, 1909, p. 11
[xli] Des Moines Register, June 15, 1909, p. 1
[xlii] Ibid
[xliii] Ibid
[xliv] Ibid
[xlv] Ibid
[xlvi] Ibid
[xlvii] Muscatine News Tribune (Muscatine, Iowa), June 19, 1909, p. 7
[xlviii] Newspapers.com
[xlix] Fargo Forum and Daily Republican, January 20, 1909, p. 3

Chapter 2

[l] Sioux City Journal, September 16, 1909, p. 9
[li] Oklahoma City Daily Pointer, September 16, 1909, p. 4
[lii] Buffalo Courier, November 14, 1909, p. 49
[liii] Chicago Tribune, November 7, 1909, p. 27
[liv] Chicago Tribune, November 10, 1909, p. 12
[lv] Ibid
[lvi] Ibid
[lvii] Ibid
[lviii] Ibid
[lix] Ibid, p. 1
[lx] Buffalo Courier, November 16, 1909, p. 1
[lxi] Rock Island Argus, November 26, 1909, p. 3
[lxii] Ibid
[lxiii] Ibid

Chapter 3

[lxiv] The Daily Times (Davenport, Iowa), December 15, 1909, p. 10
[lxv] Ibid
[lxvi] Star Tribune (Minneapolis, Minnesota), December 17, 1919, p. 10
[lxvii] Ibid
[lxviii]lxviii] Ibid
[lxix] Ibid
[lxx] Ibid
[lxxi] Ibid
[lxxii] Ibid
[lxxiii] Ibid
[lxxiv] Ottumwa Tri-Weekly Courier, December 25, 1919, p. 5
[lxxv] Ibid
[lxxvi] Ibid
[lxxvii] Ibid
[lxxviii] Ibid
[lxxix] Ibid
[lxxx] The Times (Munster, Indiana), December 28, 1909, p. 3
[lxxxi] Buffalo Courier, January 2, 1910, p. 45
[lxxxii] Ibid
[lxxxiii] Ibid
[lxxxiv] Ibid
[lxxxv] Ibid
[lxxxvi] Ibid
[lxxxvii] Ibid
[lxxxviii] The Times (Munster, Indiana), January 8, 1910, p. 3
[lxxxix] The lineage of the American Heavyweight Wrestling Championship is difficult to determine. Champions lost matches but still claimed the title. The title was vacant at times without a clear successor or match to determine the new champion. As an example, Cutler defended the American Heavyweight Championship in 1915. Stecher won but fans recognized Stecher as the World Champion. The American Title was vacant until 1917, when Wladek Zbyszko claimed it.
[xc] Rock Island Argus (Rock Island, Illinois), January 11, 1910, p. 3

[xci] Star-Gazette (Elmira, New York), January 18, 1910, p. 8
[xcii] Ibid
[xciii] Ibid
[xciv] The Baltimore Sun, January 23, 1910, p. 10
[xcv] Star Tribune (Minneapolis, Minnesota), February 4, 1910, p. 9
[xcvi] Ibid
[xcvii] Ibid
[xcviii] Star Tribune, February 15, 1910, p. 10
[xcix] Gotch vs. Hackenschmidt by the Author
[c] Star Tribune, February 15, 1910, p. 10
[ci] Ibid
[cii] Ibid
[ciii] Ibid
[civ] Ibid

Chapter 4

[cv] La Crosse Tribune (La Crosse, Wisconsin), March 10, 1910, p. 8
[cvi] Leavenworth Post (Leavenworth, Kansas), March 16, 1910, p. 7
[cvii] Chicago Tribune, March 23, 1910, p. 14
[cviii] Ibid
[cix] Buffalo Courier, March 27, 1910, p. 45
[cx] Ibid
[cxi] Ibid
[cxii] Herald and Review (Decatuer, Illinois), March 31, 1910, p. 5
[cxiii] Ibid
[cxiv] Ibid
[cxv] April 1, 1910, p. 16
[cxvi] Ibid
[cxvii] Ibid
[cxviii] Pittston Gazette (Pittston, Pennsylvania), April 14, 1910, p. 8
[cxix] The Evening News (Wilkes-Barre, Pennsylvania), April 22, 1910, p. 12
[cxx] Ibid

[cxxi] I covered this tournament extensively in Masked Marvel to the Rescue: The Gimmick That Saved the 1915 International Wrestling Tournament.
[cxxii] Republican and Herald (Pottsville, Pennsylvania), April 28, 1910, p. 2
[cxxiii] Ibid
[cxxiv] Pittsburgh Daily Post, April 30, 1910, p. 9
[cxxv] Ibid
[cxxvi] Ibid
[cxxvii] The Buffalo Enquirer (Buffalo, New York), May 2, 1910, p. 8
[cxxviii] Ibid
[cxxix] Wilkes-Barre Times Leader, May 5, 1910, p. 8
[cxxx] Ibid
[cxxxi] Ibid
[cxxxii] Ibid
[cxxxiii] Chicago Tribune, May 29, 1910, p. 24
[cxxxiv] Ibid
[cxxxv] Chicago Tribune, May 17, 1910, p. 13
[cxxxvi\] Ibid
[cxxxvii] Ibid
[cxxxviii] Ibid
[cxxxix] Ibid
[cxl] Chicago Tribune, May 14, 1910, p. 3
[cxli] Chicago Tribune, May 20, 1910, p. 4
[cxlii] Chicago Tribune, May 22, 1910, p. 1
[cxliii] Ibid
[cxliv] St. Louis Post-Dispatch, May 30, 1910, p. 10
[cxlv] Ibid
[cxlvi] Ibid

Chapter 5
[cxlvii] Chicago Tribune, March 1, 1910, p. 15
[cxlviii] Ibid
[cxlix] Ibid
[cl] Ibid
[cli] Ibid
[clii] Ibid

[cliii] The Calumet News (Calumet, Michigan), May 14, 1910, p. 2
[cliv] Ibid
[clv] Ibid
[clvi] Ibid
[clvii] Ibid
[clviii] Ibid
[clix] Chicago Tribune, June 2, 1910, p. 13
[clx] Rock Island Argus, June 2, 1910, p. 3
[clxi] Ibid
[clxii] Chicago Tribune, June 2, 1910, p. 13
[clxiii] Ibid
[clxiv] Ibid
[clxv] Chicago Tribune, June 2, 1910, p. 13 and Rock Island Argus, June 2, 1910, p. 3
[clxvi] Chicago Tribune, June 2, 1910, p. 13
[clxvii] Ibid
[clxviii] Ibid
[clxix] Ibid
[clxx] Ibid
[clxxi] Ibid
[clxxii] Ibid
[clxxiii] Ibid
[clxxiv] Ibid
[clxxv] Ibid
[clxxvi] Ibid
[clxxvii] Ibid

Chapter 6

[clxxviii] Topeka State Journal, December 29, 1910, p. 5
[clxxix] Ibid
[clxxx] Ibid
[clxxxi] Evansville Press (Evansville, Indiana), January 7, 1911, p. 1
[clxxxii] Ogden Standard (Ogden, Utah), January 12, 1911, p. 5
[clxxxiii] Gotch vs. Hackenschmidt
[clxxxiv] Santa Cruz Sentinel (Santa Cruz, California), March 26, 1911, p. 4

Chapter 7

[clxxxv] Evening Star (Washington, DC), November 1, 1910, p. 16
[clxxxvi] Ibid
[clxxxvii] Ibid
[clxxxviii] Fulton County News (McCollensburg, Pennsylvania), November 17, 1910, p. 6
[clxxxix] Wilkes-Barre Times Leader, November 10, 1910, p. 15
[cxc] Ibid
[cxci] The Boston Globe, December 3, 1910, p. 6
[cxcii] Ibid
[cxciii] The Bridgeport Times and Evening Farmer, December 15, 1910, p. 7
[cxciv] Ibid
[cxcv] Ibid
[cxcvi] Ibid
[cxcvii] Ibid
[cxcviii] Ibid
[cxcix] Ibid
[cc] Ibid
[cci] Ibid
[ccii] Ibid
[cciii] The Washington Times, January 3, 1911, p. 13
[cciv] Ibid
[ccv] Ibid
[ccvi] The Bridgeport Times and Evening Farmer, January 12, 1911, p. 7
[ccvii] Ibid
[ccviii] Ibid
[ccix] Ibid
[ccx] Ibid
[ccxi] The Lake County Times (Hammond, Indiana), January 24, 1911, p. 3
[ccxii] Ibid
[ccxiii] The Buffalo Times, January 28, 1911, p. 6
[ccxiv] Ibid
[ccxv] The Evening Times (Grand Forks, North Dakota), February 4, 1911, p.3
[ccxvi] Gotch vs. Hackenschmidt by the author

ccxvii The San Francisco Call, February 10, 1911, p. 13
ccxviii Ibid
ccxix Ibid
ccxx Ibid

Chapter 8
ccxxi Double-Crossing the Gold Dust Trio (1921) by author
ccxxii Star-Gazette (Elmira, New York), March 1, 1911, p. 8
ccxxiii Lincoln Journal Star (Lincoln, Nebraska), March 7, 1911, p. 6
ccxxiv Ibid
ccxxv Ibid
ccxxvi Arizona Republican (Phoenix, Arizona), March 16, 1911, p. 1
ccxxvii Ibid
ccxxviii Ibid
ccxxix Detroit Free Press, March 19, 1911, p. 22
ccxxx Ibid
ccxxxi Ibid
ccxxxii Ibid
ccxxxiii Ibid
ccxxxiv Ibid
ccxxxv Norwich Bulletin (Norwich, Connecticut), March 30, 1911, p. 1.
ccxxxvi Rock Island Argus (Rock Island, Illinois), May 24, 1911, p. 3

Chapter 9
ccxxxvii The Lake County Times (Hammond, Indiana), September 21, 1911, p. 3
ccxxxviii Bridgeport Evening Farmer (Bridgeport, Connecticut), October 23, 1911, p. 7
ccxxxix Ibid
ccxl Ibid
ccxli Ibid
ccxlii The Detroit Times, October 28, 1911, p. 2
ccxliii The Bridgeport Evening Farmer, December 18, 1911, p. 8

[ccxliv] Times Union (Brooklyn, New York), December 26, 1911, p. 8
[ccxlv] The Bridgeport Evening Farmer, December 26, 1911, p. 7
[ccxlvi] Times Union (Brooklyn, New York), December 26, 1911, p. 8
[ccxlvii] Ibid
[ccxlviii] Ibid
[ccxlix] Ibid
[ccl] Ibid
[ccli] Ibid
[cclii] Ibid
[ccliii] Ibid
[ccliv] The Detroit Times, December 27, 1911, p. 4
[cclv] Evening Journal (Wilmington, Delaware), January 1, 1912, p. 7
[cclvi] The Detroit Times, December 28, 1911, p. 6
[cclvii] Salt Lake Tribune (Salt Lake City, Utah), January 11, 1912, p. 10
[cclviii] Ibid
[cclix] Ibid
[cclx] Ibid
[cclxi] Ibid
[cclxii] Ibid
[cclxiii] Ibid
[cclxiv] Star Tribune (Minneapolis, Minnesota), January 17, 1912, p. 11
[cclxv] Ibid
[cclxvi] Ibid
[cclxvii] Ibid
[cclxviii] Ibid
[cclxix] Ibid
[cclxx] Ibid
[cclxxi] The Fairmont West Virginian (Fairmont, West Virginia), February 7, 1912, p. 6
[cclxxii] Ibid
[cclxxiii] New York Tribune, February 13, 1912, p. 8
[cclxxiv] Ibid
[cclxxv] Ibid

[cclxxvi] Ibid
[cclxxvii] Ibid
[cclxxviii] Ibid
[cclxxix] Ibid
[cclxxx] Ibid
[cclxxxi] Ibid
[cclxxxii] Ibid
[cclxxxiii] Ibid
[cclxxxiv] The Washington Herald (Washington, D.C.), March 11, 1912, p. 8
[cclxxxv] Salt Lake Tribune (Salt Lake City, Utah), March 22, 1912, p. 6
[cclxxxvi] Ibid

Chapter 10
[cclxxxvii] Frank Gotch, World Champion Wrestler by George Sanders Robbins, p. 23
[cclxxxviii] Ibid
[cclxxxix] Ibid
[ccxc] Ibid
[ccxci] Ibid
[ccxcii] Georg Lurich at wrestlingdata.com
[ccxciii] The Kansas City Times (Kansas City, Missouri), April 2, 1913, p. 1
[ccxciv] Ibid
[ccxcv] Ibid
[ccxcvi] Ibid
[ccxcvii] Ibid
[ccxcviii] Ibid
[ccxcix] Ibid
[ccc] Ibid

Chapter 11
[ccci] The Boston Globe, May 26, 1913, p. 4
[cccii] Brooklyn Daily Eagle, May 29, 1913, p. 20
[ccciii] Ibid
[coiv] Ibid
[cccv] Ibid

[cccvi] The 1915 New York International Wrestling Tournament consisted of a spring and a fall tournament. I cover the tournament in-depth in *Masked Marvel to the Rescue: The Gimmick That Saved the 1915 New York International Tournament* (2020).
[cccvii] The Boston Globe, February 27, 1914, p. 6
[cccviii] Ibid
[cccix] Ibid
[cccx] Ibid
[cccxi] Ibid
[cccxii] Ibid
[cccxiii] San Francisco Examiner, May 2, 1917, p. 15
[cccxiv] The Bemidji Daily Pioneer (Bemidji, Minnesota), May 16, 1914, p. 1
[cccxv] Ibid
[cccxvi] Ibid
[cccxvii] Ibid
[cccxviii] Dakota County Herald (Dakota City, Nebraska), November 12, 1914, p. 7
[cccxix] Masked Marvel to the Rescue by author

Conclusion
[cccxx] P. 168. Completely ignoring that Gotch allowed Zbyszko five percent of the first gate, hardly a windfall.
[cccxxi] The Evening Times (Grand Forks, North Dakota), March 6, 1912, p. 3

Epilogue
[cccxxii] Ogden Standard (Ogden, Utah), October 17, 1917, p. 1
[cccxxiii] Alaska Daily Empire (Juneau, Alaska), October 29, 1917, p. 3
[cccxxiv] Chicago Eagle, November 10, 1917, p. 9
[cccxxv] Ibid
[cccxxvi] Ibid
[cccxxvii] The Daily Times (Davenport, Iowa), December 17, 1917, p. 1

www.ingramcontent.com/pod-product-compliance
Lightning Source LLC
LaVergne TN
LVHW021707060526
838200LV00050B/2549

9 781088 130261